For Debbie
Thank
you
Alpha
Blessings,
Gail
Stand Firm
Heb. 6:19

A Firm Place to Stand

Finding Ultimate Security in an Insecure World

By Gail E. Rodgers

 FriesenPress

One Printers Way
Altona, MB R0G 0B0
Canada

www.friesenpress.com

Photo credits: Rodgers Family Photo Album

ISBN
978-1-03-831503-8 (Hardcover)
978-1-03-831502-1 (Paperback)
978-1-03-831504-5 (eBook)

1. RELIGION, CHRISTIAN LIVING, SPIRITUAL GROWTH

Distributed to the trade by The Ingram Book Company

For my family, with love

"One generation commends your works to another; they tell of your mighty acts. They speak of the glorious splendor of Your majesty."
Psalm 145: 4 & 5 (NIV)

TABLE OF CONTENTS

<u>*Acknowledgements*</u>

*With gratitude to Patricia A. Psooy
for her many hours of dedication in mining out and compil-
ing the names of God and what they reveal in Scripture.
She inspired my search.*

*Thank you to my supportive family and especially to my
dear husband, John, for being my greatest cheerleader
through all of life.*

*Thank you to my special friend for editing,
and to my dear friends who read, cared and prayed.
I am grateful for you all.*

*"Those who know your name will trust in you,
for you, LORD,
have never forsaken those who seek you."
Psalm 9:10 (NIV)*

What a treasure it is to explore the nature of the LORD GOD ALMIGHTY wrapped up in the names of

The mystery of this Three-in-One God, **The Holy Trinity,** though individual in relationship, is intermingled in character and works in harmony to draw us into relationship with this divine mystery of love.

Though we cannot fully understand it; by faith we can enter this place of security where we are encased in the fullness of "The Trinity", sometimes called the "Godhead".

The depth of this love draws us to God's presence, Jesus Christ's peace and the Holy Spirit's power to live encased in this refuge. This is a firm place to stand, in a security that is strong, firm and steadfast. We can be encased in His presence to participate in the immeasurable fullness of God!

THE HOLY TRINITY

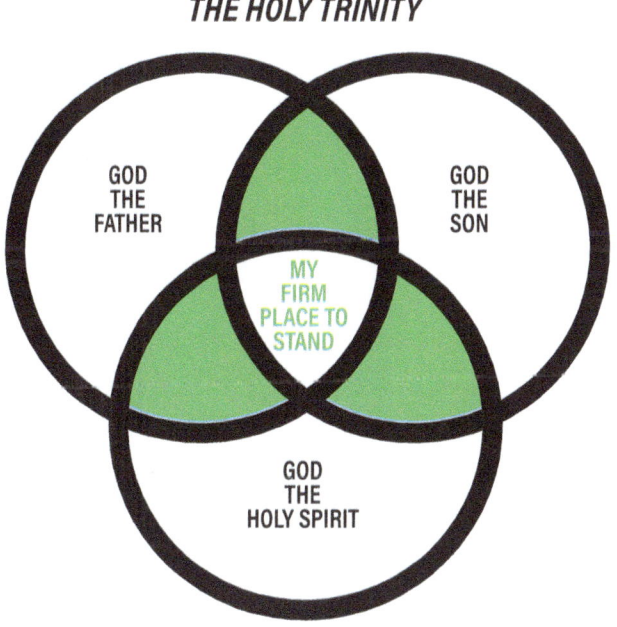

GOD THE FATHER

GOD THE SON

MY FIRM PLACE TO STAND

GOD THE HOLY SPIRIT

Preface

We all encounter times of confusion, chaos and questioning when the fog just doesn't seem to lift and the way forward is obscured, leaving us feeling shaky.

We try to encourage one another as we step toward the unknown. Yet our hearts feel the weight of the questions, the insecurities we try to navigate.

We all know how stress affects our physical, emotional and spiritual well-being. We feel it when uncertainty presents itself. Our thoughts feel tangled; our stomachs tighten, and our sense of God can feel distant.

The more stress we have, the less capacity we have for anyone or anything else. The more peace we have, the more room we have for others and for our pursuit of God and the security He can bring to our hearts and minds.

We all want to thrive, not just "get by" or feel as if we are simply "surviving". But what does it take, in this hour, to thrive as a follower of Jesus amidst the questions we experience daily? How do we find that firm place to stand when things feel uncertain or shaken? This series is a collection of snapshots from my life as I have camped on this very question.

GOD'S NAMES. GOD'S NATURE. GOD'S PROMISES.

Camping on **the names of God as Father, Son and Holy Spirit** anchors me as I begin to see His character emerge more clearly. As I rest in who He is, I find an amazing place of security and fullness. It is a place of peace that passes all understanding, where we get fresh glimpses of our Great God, our ultimate security in this insecure world. He encases us, wraps us in His presence where we are sheltered in our inner being. Peace arises within as we see the length, width and depth of His love for us. Strength and thanksgiving arise as we anchor in this firm place.

We need to hear the stories of one another's glimpses of God. This is mine. I hope it inspires you to tell your stories and to seek new glimpses of Him as we navigate an ever-changing landscape. Finding our security and stability in our Great God, this firm place to stand, fills us with joy and in His presence, we become fully alive.

CHAPTER ONE

FINDING A FIRM PLACE TO STAND

GOD'S NAMES. GOD'S NATURE. GOD'S PROMISES.

CHAPTER ONE

Finding A Firm Place to Stand

Section One

Why the names of God matter

A Little Background

As a child I was taught about God. He was big and mysterious yet loving and kind. He was a miracle worker, a promise keeper whom I could talk to anytime, anywhere, about anything. My young heart was filled with awe.

As an adult, I encountered others who believed this way, but also many who didn't. Some of my friends abandoned their faith in God. They felt there were too many unanswered prayers, too much guilt or judgment from other Christians. The picture of the loving God they had been taught became tarnished with disappointment and hurt. Some felt they had grown past the simplicity of the story of God's love.

I had my own questions too. Many of my own "grocery list" prayers of earnest "Please! Please!" didn't result in the answers I had thought were promised. I began to realize I didn't really know much about God. He is a mystery too great to fathom. Yet the Bible does paint a picture that helps us get a glimpse of Him. And that glimpse can be life changing.

My friend Patricia Psooy, a keen follower of Jesus, has spent decades combing the Bible to try to understand the character of God. She dove into the various names of God and what they revealed about Him. Like pieces of a vast puzzle, these names help us catch a glimpse of our great God through the stories of the Bible and through our own encounters.

As I ponder these Scriptures, my picture of who God is enlarges. I know I have barely scratched the surface of His vastness. Yet, as I camp on who He is as "God the Father", "God the Son" and "God the Holy Spirit," my reverence and awe can't help but expand!

As my heart settles into this mysterious depth of who He is, I find my prayers changing and my confidence in God deepening.

We all carry our own questions of this mystery. Sharing the journey reminds me of the glowing fire when the logs are stacked together. If one log rolls away from the rest, isolated, it quickly loses its warmth and glow. As we hear each other's stories and recount our glimpses, we spur one another on in the warmth of God's love for us, even in a cold world.

Trying to grasp the awesomeness of God through the mystery of the Trinity, feels a bit like trying to capture Niagara Falls in a teacup. We capture a glimpse, a few drops, and it is only just a taste, a refreshing that will leave us wanting more. It reminds me of Psalm 34:8 (NIV).

"Taste and see that the LORD is good.
Blessed is the one who takes refuge in Him."

We all daily navigate a world where the names God and Jesus have become merely exclamation marks, sometimes expletives, with little or no thought of who He is. Yet within those very names there is revealed power, protection and peace that can anchor us.

As we delve into who He is through His names, He enables us to trust Him, to discover His love in new and personal ways. He invites us into this security, this refuge, this firm place to stand through the turbulence of life.

"Those who know your name will trust in you,
for you, LORD, have never forsaken those who seek you."
Psalm 9:10 (NIV)

Our world is a wonder of natural beauty that feeds our souls. Yet it is also a world of contradictions, division and confusion. We can find ourselves feeling adrift, flat, unsure when questions abound. It can be easy to feel God is distant, uninterested and silent as we navigate our day-to-day challenges. We can begin to frame His presence in our lives with words that express doubt, disappointment or discouragement in our walk with Him. And our prayers can feel as if they hit the ceiling.

As we get to know who our God is; as we discover His nature and all He has promised to be for us as we trust Him, we find something happens within us.

Our faith grows.
Our love grows.
Our confidence in God Himself grows.
And our place of peace enlarges.

We get to know God as so much more than just a distant being we call on when we press the panic button in life. Amid the noise and chaos, we are invited to a place of security and quiet rest, a place of peace.

A place of Celebration!

When we are missing PEACE,
Knowing God is the missing PIECE.

Section Two

The Invitation

God's invitation is to step out of the noise and find rest. Oh, it is not so much a physical rest like a long nap or a good night's sleep. The invitation is to find rest within our very being.

- Rest for our minds from the constant attempts to problem solve.

- Rest for our emotions that feel the demands of the hour.

- Rest from desperate pleading prayers for God to change our circumstances.

- Even rest in our choices and decisions that can leave us 'scrolling' with that "I don't know what to do" feeling.

> The Bible calls it "rest for your soul".
> A place to anchor in peace daily.
> A place to shelter when turbulence rolls in.

God offers us rest for our souls. It is rest at the very heart of who we are, rest from the very heart of who He is ... even in spite of what is happening around us. Here's the invitation to team up with Him in Jesus' own words,

"Come to me, all you who are weary and burdened, and I will give you rest. Take my yoke upon you and learn from me, for I am gentle and humble in heart, and you will find rest for your souls." Matthew 11:28-30 (NIV).

The Message paraphrase puts it this way:

"Are you tired? Worn out? Burned out on religion? Come to me. Get away with me and you'll recover your life. I'll show you how to take a real rest. Walk with me and work with me—watch how I do it. Learn the unforced rhythms of

grace. I won't lay anything heavy or ill-fitting on you. Keep company with me and you'll learn to live freely and lightly." -Jesus - Matthew 11:28-30 The Message.

What a wonderful invitation!

PAUSE & PONDER

What words would you use to frame God's presence in your life?

Does His invitation stir your heart?

The Invitation is to "Come"

The Father calls us.
"Come, let's talk."

*"My heart has heard you say, "Come and talk with Me".
And my heart responds,
"LORD, I am coming"." Psalm 27:8 (NLT)*

The Son says, "Come. Rest."

*"Come to Me all you who are weary and
heavy burdened
and I will give you rest... for your souls."
Matthew 11:28 & 29 (NIV)*

The Spirit whispers, "Come. Learn."

*"The Advocate, the Holy Spirit, whom the Father will
send in
My name, will teach you all things..." John 14:26 (NIV)*

It is in responding to the invitation that we find this rest. We accept the invitation ...

- through faith in God.
- through belief in Jesus' death and resurrection.
- through receiving the empowerment of the Holy Spirit.

When we give our firm "Yes!" to God's invitation, we experience peace **WITH** God and the peace *OF* God enters our inner being. He awaits our response.

"LORD, I am coming."

As we respond to God's invitation, He brings us into the powerhouse of THE TRINITY.

PAUSE & PONDER

Does my heart respond, "LORD, I am coming"?

If I have never responded to the LORD's nudge at my heart's door, am I ready to say "Yes"?

God's love and presence comes to rescue us just where we are, even in the middle of a crisis or a mess, even when we feel in the pit, and especially when we feel in the pit.

Jesus' grace comes to redeem us. Accepting us just as we are, knowing the best of us and the worst of us, He offers us His peace and His restoration. He lifts us from the pit.

The Holy Spirit comes to transform us as He **reveals** God's power in us to live fully alive, strong, firm and steadfast!

"I waited patiently for the LORD; he turned to me and heard my cry.

He lifted me out of the slimy pit, out of the mud and mire;
he set my feet on a rock and gave me a firm place to stand.

He put a new song in my mouth, a hymn of praise to our God. Many will see and fear the LORD and put their trust in Him."

Psalm 40:1-3 (NIV)

The Hebrew word translated as "fear" in this verse is "yirah", meaning awe: beholding something that fills us with wonder, with deep respect, a sense of the majestic; filled with reverence and worship. It is connected to trembling in awe.

When we step into the invitation of God's love, Jesus' grace and the Holy Spirit's power it is an awesome place, a place of wonder. The "new song of praise to our God" that is referred to in Psalm 40:1-3, begins to bubble up within us as we move out of the mud and mire to firm footing, filled with awe in this new place of His presence.

All of God is available to all of me!

And ... our prayers begin to change!

As I "pitch my tent" in this firm place of awe I find my prayers changing. The desperate prayers of "Please God, please!" begging Him to change the circumstances, begin to move to confident prayers of "Thank you! Thank you!". Prayers of thanksgiving to God for all He is as He empowers me within my very being, right where I walk, leave me strengthened and thirsty for more of Him.

PAUSE & PONDER

God's heart of love is to rescue us, redeem us and reveal Himself to us. His names mark the dot-to-dot pictures that reveal His goodness, His love and the mystery of His majesty!

"LORD, fill my vision, my heart and mind with awe of You. Forgive me for the times I take You for granted or keep You small and marginalized in my life. Please help me to remember that all I need today, I will find in You. Help me to run to You in times of confusion and hurt and not away from You. Thank you for this firm place to stand. In the strong name of Jesus I pray. Amen.

Section Three

The Bible Points the Way

In the Old Testament story of Moses, when he was being asked by God to lead the Israelites out of bondage and to freedom, he wanted to say no. He told God he was too inadequate to answer His call. God replied:

"My presence will go with you, and I will give you rest".
Exodus 33:14 (NIV)

God's presence accompanied Moses every step of his journey as he did indeed lead the people to freedom from captivity.

God's Father heart to rescue His people and give His presence is still our promise today. The Old Testament stories remind us of the constant call of God to return our hearts to Him. These stories point to the coming Jesus. Out of God's great love He planned to send His Presence through Jesus.

God the Father promised His PRESENCE

In the New Testament of the Bible, before Jesus was cruelly crucified, He was comforting His disciples. He knew of the coming miracle of His resurrection, but His followers did not. They were troubled by the circumstances of the day and of Jesus' talk of leaving them. He promised:

"Peace I leave with you; my peace I give you. I do not give to you as the world gives. Do not let your hearts be troubled and do not be afraid." John 14:27 (NIV)

Jesus, our Redeemer, promised to buy back our troubled and broken hearts through His death and resurrection. Today, out of His great love, Jesus still offers this indescribable gift of peace to those who believe in Him and say "Yes!" to His invitation to "come" and accept this gift of love.

God the Son promises His PEACE

Jesus also promised that when He left the earth, God would send the Holy Spirit to be an Advocate for Jesus' followers. He would defend and support them; help, comfort, strengthen and bring them wisdom, revelation and divine power. All who ask and believe will receive this gift of the power of the Holy Spirit.

"But you will receive power when the Holy Spirit comes on you; and you will be my witnesses in Jerusalem, and in all Judea and Samaria, and to the ends of the earth." Acts 1:8 (NIV)

The Holy Spirit is still available today, in all His power, to those who ask Him to fill them.

God the Holy Spirit promises us His POWER

We have 24/7 access to this peace, this place of security, this power! It is never ending, always available for us.

Run your finger around the Trinity symbol. There is no beginning and no end. The well of all He is never dries up. Every time we put our bucket down in this secure place, fresh power and wisdom is there to be drawn on from this amazing God.

This Three-in-One mystery gives us this firm place to stand, encasing us...

In the amazing presence and love of God.

In the unexplainable peace of Jesus Christ.

With access to the miraculous power of the Holy Spirit.

What a cause for rejoicing and praise!
What a celebration!

GOD THE FATHER

GOD THE HOLY SPIRIT

HIS PRESENCE

GOD THE SON

HE INVITES ME

HIS POWER

HIS PEACE

HIS WORD PROCLAIMS IT

"Through Christ Jesus we have also obtained access by faith into this grace in which we now stand. And we rejoice in the hope of the glory of God." Romans 5:2 (NIV)

"For through him (Christ) we both have access to the Father by one Spirit." Ephesians 2:18 (NIV)

"Therefore God exalted him to the highest place and gave him the name that is above every name, that at the name of Jesus every knee should bow, in heaven and on earth and under the earth, and every tongue acknowledge that Jesus Christ is Lord, to the glory of God the Father." Philippians 2:9-11 (NIV)

We are given access **by** His grace and given access **to** His grace!

We have access to God through Jesus, whose name is above every name. We have access by the power of the Holy Spirit.

SUCH A GIFT!

"If you declare with your mouth, "Jesus is Lord," and believe in your heart that God raised him from the dead, you will be saved. For it is with your heart that you believe and are justified, and it is with your mouth that you profess your faith and are saved."

Romans 10:9&10 (NIV)

PAUSE & PONDER

"LORD, I am coming!"

Thank you, LORD, that You accept me just as I am, where I am and You invite me into Your presence, Your peace and Your power. Thank you that You have given me access into this grace that You pour out on me so generously. Today I accept You by faith, believing in Your presence in my life, receiving Your much needed peace in my heart and mind, and believing in Your resurrection power that is available to me. How incredible that is!

Please open my eyes to new glimpses of You as I study Your names. Thank you for accepting me as Your child and giving me access to all of You, God the Father, God the Son and God the Holy Spirit. I receive You now...

Section Four

Baptized in The Name

If you have ever professed your faith through being baptized by water, you will recall the words, *"I baptize you in the name of The Father, and of The Son and of The Holy Spirit".*

As we are baptized into this powerhouse of who God is, we are baptized into this incredible place of access to the fullness of God! Notice the word is singular, the NAME, not plural. We are baptized into the fullness of the Trinity.

Taking this step of baptism is an important symbolic declaration of a choice to stand in this firm place, rejoicing in new life through the death and resurrection of Jesus and in the power of the Holy Spirit.

Much like a wedding ring is a symbol to the world of the commitment two people make to one another in marriage, so baptism is a symbol of our commitment to the Sovereign Lord. It is a declaration that we have accepted the invitation to believe in Jesus, to receive new life and to walk with Him in the power of His Spirit.

"Baptizing them in the name of the Father and of the Son and of the Holy Spirit." Matthew 28:19 (NIV)

A prayer from 14th century Italian author Catherine of Siena (1347 – 1386)

"You, O eternal Trinity,

are a deep sea, into which the more I enter the more I find,

and the more I find the more I seek...

O eternal Godhead,

what more could You give me than Yourself?

You are the fire that ever burns without being consumed;

You consume in Your heat all the soul's self-love.

You are the fire which takes away cold;

with Your light You illuminate me so that I may know all Your truth.

Amen"

Section Five

Making it Personal

Ephesians 3 voices a prayer we can pray as our own to be strengthened in our inner beings. Consider personalizing it with "me", "my" or "I".

"I pray that out of his glorious riches he may strengthen you with power through his Spirit in your inner being, so that Christ may dwell in your hearts through faith.

"And I pray that you, being rooted and established in love, may have power, together with all the Lord's holy people, to grasp how wide and long and high and deep is the love of Christ, and to know this love that surpasses knowledge - that you may be filled to the measure of all the fullness of God." Ephesians 3:16-19 (NIV)

What a promise it is to write on the tablet of our hearts! As we allow it to steep in our hearts and minds, as tea steeps in a pot growing stronger, His presence and power in us will grow stronger as well.

PAUSE & PONDER

"Are you tired? Worn out? Burned out on religion?

Come to me. Get away with me and you'll recover your life." Jesus

It is good to ask ourselves, "Where am I worn out these days?"

Take some time talking to God about it. Stay long enough in His presence to receive His peace.

If you feel stuck, invite Him into that area. Linger with Him.....

You can use this outline to BLESS and pray for needs in your own life or for those you care about. Listen for God's quiet voice as you pray. As we are filled with His presence, His peace and His power we are strengthened for whatever we will encounter in our day.

B- Body

L- Labor

E- Emotions

S- Social Life

S- Spiritual Life

LORD, Thank you that I can get to know You and Your power in my life as I turn to You daily. Please show me:

B - Body

- Is there anything I need to pay attention to in my physical body?

L - Labor

- Am I using my energy wisely and for what is best?

E - Emotions

- Please show me if I am harboring any emotions that I need to talk with You about and receive Your help in releasing.

S - Social Life

- Guide me in my choices of the company I keep and the entertainment that I seek.

S - Spiritual Life

- Above all, help me to guard my heart so that I can nurture Your presence in my life. I want to hear You more clearly and walk with You more closely.

Thank you that You invite me into this secure place of walking with You in all the fullness of Father, Son and Holy Spirit. Amen.

Thank you that I can bring my question marks to You, trusting You to guide me through the maze; knowing You know the way.

He Invites Me

"Come to me, all you who are weary and burdened,

and I will give you rest.

Team up with me and learn from me,

for I am gentle and humble in heart,

and you will find rest for your souls. "

Matthew 11:28&29.

THE HOLY TRINITY

GOD THE FATHER

GOD THE SON

Into His Presence

Into His Peace

HE INVITES ME

Into His Power

GOD THE HOLY SPIRIT

CHAPTER TWO

WHAT'S IN A NAME?

GOD'S NAMES. GOD'S NATURE. GOD'S PROMISES.

CHAPTER TWO

WHAT'S IN A NAME?

Section One

What is the big deal about God's names?

My Mom used to say that when God has something to say to His followers you will begin to hear it everywhere. Over her ninety-six years of paying attention to God she had seen this pattern over and over. The names of God are a popular topic these days. I believe God is calling His followers to really focus on who He is, to lift our eyes off the burdens and questions that swirl around us and to look intently at Him; focusing on all that His names reveal about His love toward us and His power within us.

A Little Background

Long before God sent Jesus to be the Redeemer for human-kind, He planned the rescue of our souls. He planned for bless-ing to return to the human race after friendship with God had been broken in the Garden of Eden. He planned for restoration to replace the brokenness that life so often brings from our own self-absorption and the self-focus of others. We all know how life can be wonderful on many levels, yet wearing and challenging too, leaving us weary, burdened and empty. God's heart of love planned the renewal of fellowship between God and us. He planned on sending Jesus to bridge the divide.

In the book of Isaiah, the coming of Jesus is foretold. God's rescue plan. Isaiah 7:14 (NIV) tells us, *"Therefore the Lord himself will give you a sign: The virgin will be with child and will give birth to a son and will call him **Immanuel.**"*

As the coming of this child was prophesied, He was also described.

"For unto us a Child is born, unto us a Son is given; And the government will be upon His shoulders. And His name will be called Wonderful, Counselor, Mighty God, Everlasting Father, Prince of Peace." *Isaiah 9:6 (NKJV)*

Do you hear God the Father, God the Son and God the Holy Spirit all being described in this foretelling of His coming? Yet the word "name" is singular.

"Mighty God" and "Everlasting Father". Jesus, the "Prince of Peace".
And "Wonderful, Counselor", describing the Holy Spirit.

In Matthew 1:23 the prophesy from Isaiah 7 is repeated and continues with an interpretation of the name, Immanuel. (The "I" or "E" spelling is simply a variation between the Hebrew and the Greek of the old and new testaments.)

"A virgin will be with child and will give birth to a son, and they shall call him Immanuel" - which means, "God with us".
Matthew 1:23 (NIV)

God with us!

What a beautiful expression of The Trinity, our three-in-one God! The names foretold in the book of Isaiah give depth to all God is and all He offers us of Himself through Jesus. All of this wrapped up in the Baby Jesus we celebrate at Christmas. So much more than just a baby!

THE HOLY TRINITY

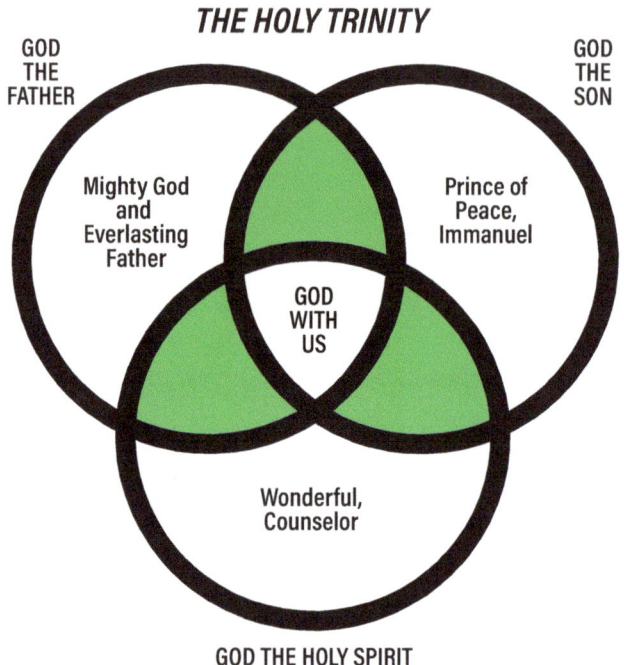

GOD
THE
FATHER

GOD
THE
SON

Mighty God
and
Everlasting
Father

Prince of
Peace,
Immanuel

GOD
WITH
US

Wonderful,
Counselor

GOD THE HOLY SPIRIT

"Thanks be to God for his indescribable gift!"
2 Corinthians 9:15 (NIV)

Do you know the meaning of your name? In Western culture we tend to name children with names we simply like, or names of parents or grandparents. In Biblical times a name was often significant in reflecting events surrounding a birth, or chosen to reflect a blessing, a character trait or a hope for the child. Sometimes names reflected desired characteristics like the name, "Grace". Or they held meaning such as, "brave warrior", as in the name Louis. Strong names of great leaders or Bible characters are still popular today.

The Hebrew name of God was originally considered too sacred to even speak. It was only written as YHWH. Even to write it was a task of great reverence. The writer was required to first go through a detailed ritual of cleansing, and when ready to finally write the name of God, even a fresh quill was required to dip into a fresh pot of ink.

Eventually vowels were added, creating the word YAHWEH. In English this word is translated, Jehovah or LORD of all. When we see the word LORD, in all capital letters in Scripture, it refers to YAHWEH, LORD OVERALL. He is Sovereign LORD of all! Scattered throughout the Bible are descriptions of the LORD that help us know His character. These are known as the Jehovah names of God, each revealing an aspect of who YAHWEH, Jehovah God, is.

When we read a story in the Bible and see the name of God translated as "LORD", and then read a descriptor word following, we know God is being described, or He is describing Himself, essentially saying,

"This is who I AM".

YHWH
YAHWEH

JEHOVAH
SOVEREIGN LORD OF ALL

LORD GOD ALMIGHTY

Section Two

God Reveals Himself

One of the first places in the Bible where we see God identify Himself, is in the story of Moses in the book of Exodus.

Moses had a direct encounter with the LORD when he was herding his father-in-law's sheep. The drama of his earlier life was behind him. The Israelites (his people) were still captives in Egypt.

Moses' Earlier Life

At the time of his birth, Moses' Israeli mother had received wisdom from God as to how to protect her baby boy when the Pharaoh of Egypt was intent on killing Hebrew babies. But God had plans for Moses. His mother made a basket of reeds and laid her precious baby boy in it. Then she placed it in the river very near where the Pharaoh's daughter would go to bathe. The baby's sister, Miriam, hid nearby. The Princess, the daughter of the Pharaoh, found baby Moses and insisted on keeping the sweet baby. Miriam offered to find a local woman to breastfeed the child. Of course she brought her own mother. God, in His kindness had Moses' very own mother called to nurse him and raise him until he went to the palace to live with the Princess and the Pharaoh's family.

Moses grew up seeing both worlds, the world of the wealthy Egyptians and the world of his enslaved people. His frustration at the bondage of his people turned to anger and one day he murdered an Egyptian, thinking it was in secret. But he was found out and took refuge in the land of Midian, where he settled, married and became a sheep herder for 40 years.

Moses was probably feeling life was pretty predictable as he crisscrossed the land finding the best places for the sheep to graze. His weathered skin was aging. He was probably feeling life was just a settled routine now. Certainly, he was not expecting a divine encounter. Yet, while out with the sheep one ordinary day, Moses saw a bush on fire. He noticed it did not burn up and he turned aside to investigate. He heard his name called twice. "Moses, Moses".

He knew it was the LORD speaking and he replied, **"Here I am."**
Exodus 3:4 (NIV)

Then God instructed him not to come any closer to the burning bush, but to, "take off your sandals, you are standing on holy ground". Moses hid his face; he knew he was encountering the holiness of God. God told him, *"I am the God of your fathers, Abraham, Isaac and Jacob."*

Moses knew of the covenant God had made with his ancestors, Abraham, his son Isaac and then to Isaac's son, Jacob. The promise was that one-day God would return the land to the Israelites and that the promised Messiah would one day come through the line of Abraham.

God is a covenant keeping God, a promise keeper. The covenant He initiated with Abraham to rescue the Israelites was a foreshadowing, an arrow pointing to His coming new covenant of grace to us, through the Messiah, Jesus.

Back at the burning bush it became clear to Moses that God was calling *him* to lead the people out of bondage in Egypt. God was calling Moses to be His spokesman. God's intention was to deliver the Israelites from the hands of the Egyptians. God was on a mission of compassion to rescue the Israelites. This was again the arrow, the foreshadowing of God's compassionate rescue mission to all of us through the coming of Jesus.

Moses was reluctant and offered excuses, even though God promised to be with him. Finally ... Moses asked God,

"Suppose I go to the Israelites and say to them, 'The God of your fathers has sent me to you,' and they ask me, 'What is his name?' Then what shall I tell them?"

"God said to Moses ***"I AM WHO I AM.***
This is what you are to say to the Israelites:
'I AM' has sent me to you.'"
Exodus 3:13-14 (NIV)

When God calls Himself, **"I AM"** in this text in Exodus, this is reference to the amazing character of YAHWEH, LORD of all! He is the one who planned the rescue of the Israelites, and the One who planned our rescue from our own brokenness. As He was in the past, He still is today, and He will be in eternity;

worthy of our holy, highest regard, worthy of all our trust, worthy of all our praise!

All through Scripture **"I AM"** is followed by words that describe pictures of who God is. All through the Old Testament these descriptors help us understand Him as **God the Father.**

In the New Testament **"I AM"** is also used in seven declarations Jesus used to describe Himself in the Gospels. These help us understand Him as **God the Son.**

God the Holy Spirit is also described with names and characteristics sprinkled throughout the Bible. The "Spirit of the Lord" is described in Isaiah 11:1-3 pointing to the Holy Spirit, who would be the One sent at Pentecost after Jesus' return to Heaven.

The God who created the galaxies, the depth of the oceans and the mysteries of science, desires to reveal Himself to us, to you and to me in all His splendor ... as our three-in-One God. What an incredible thought that is! He is the LORD of all!

"I AM"!

"God with us!"

God, the great "I AM" of the Old Testament, declared Himself the "Eternal God". (Genesis 21:33) "Everlasting". Through the ages His love would never stop. His various names reveal His loving nature and His desire to **RESCUE** humanity. His names point to Jesus, continuing the love story of God and His mission to reconcile humanity to Himself, to walk and talk with us again as He did in the garden of Eden before the greed of knowledge and independence from God broke the relationship.

Jesus, through His own declarations of "I AM" throughout the Gospels, declares Himself the Messiah who was foretold in the Old Testament. His character and heart is to **REDEEM** our broken places as we put our faith in His death and resurrection and receive His restoration.

The Holy Spirit's character is shown through the traits and gifts the Bible promises He will bring to our inner being, infusing us with His power and **REVEALING** the way to freedom from the bondage of fear and all the things that hold us captive.

This amazing love of God for us, woven throughout the Bible through the picture of our three-in-one God, **THE TRINITY**, is something we can rely on! We can rely on His love as we stand in this firm place.

As we embrace who the eternal God is,
opening our hearts to Jesus, the Messiah, through faith,
He empowers us by the Holy Spirit!

"And so we know and rely on the love God has for us.
God is love.
Whoever lives in love lives in God, and God in him."
1 John 4:16 (NIV)

This love is reliable!

There are some incredible verses in the Bible that detail this firm place, this strength in our inner beings, through The Trinity.

God the Father pours his love and acceptance out to us from His storehouse of glorious riches. He extends the invitation to restored relationship with Him. **The Rescuer.**

Jesus Christ takes up residence within us, at our invitation, so that we can actually dwell in this place of being rooted and established in this amazing, reliable love. **The Redeemer**.

The Holy Spirit infuses our inner beings with power, to be transformed as He draws us to faith in Jesus and empowers us to walk in that faith. **The Revealer.**

> *"I have not stopped giving thanks for you, remembering you in my prayers. I keep asking that the God of our Lord Jesus Christ, the glorious Father, may give you the Spirit of wisdom and revelation, so that you may know Him better.*
>
> *"I pray also that the eyes of your heart may be enlightened in order that you may know the hope to which he has called you, the riches of his glorious inheritance in the saints, and his incomparably great power for us who believe." Ephesians 1:16-19 (NIV) - Paul to the church.*

God instructs us to do this together, powerfully grasping this indescribable love that surpasses our knowledge. We need each other's stories of His faithful love holding us firm. Just as the logs in the fireplace keep each other burning brightly, while the isolated log grows cold, so we need one another in order to be encouraged to stay close to the flame.

"But encourage one another daily, as long as it is called "Today", so that none of you may be hardened by sin's deceitfulness." Hebrews 3:13 (NIV)

PAUSE & PONDER

Who are the people I can connect with to encourage me in my walk with God? Do I sense any hardness creeping into my own heart?

Where can I make an effort to be together with those who will strengthen me as I trust God; helping me to establish my relationship with Jesus and walk in the power of the Holy Spirit?

 FATHER  SON  HOLY SPIRIT

Section Three

A snapshot from our album of life

In Winds of Uncertainty

We had just moved to the little mining town in the far North. There were no roads in or out, only an airstrip. Our mobile home nestled on the shore of a beautiful lake surrounded by forest. It was tranquil, serene and lovely. We had just signed our names to a large loan, purchasing a share in the small air service that serviced the area. John, my pilot husband would manage the operation of several single and twin-engine aircraft. He was flying, fixing, managing pilots, hauling groceries, patients, geologists, teachers and a host of other people and things required to live in the isolated communities scattered around this remote region. I would run the office, a large porch on the side of our mobile home. My days were filled with booking and tracking the aircraft, keeping an ear tuned all day to the two-way radio connecting planes and communities, doing books, keeping the coffee hot on very cold days and managing our home and two small children. We were excited to settle in and looked forward to our future there. We loved northern living!

One of the personal items we had taken along in the limited boxes we could bring was a wooden plaque on which John had inscribed Psalm 37:5. It was the verse we had claimed as our own when we were engaged. We would trust the LORD with our journey through life and commit our way continually to Him.

> **"Commit your way unto the LORD,**
> **trust also in him and**
> **he shall bring it to pass."**
> **Psalm 37:5 (KJV)**

As I hung it on the wall in our new home, we had little idea of how we would be called on to trust the LORD in this place.

Before we could even get our boxes unpacked, a major announcement from the mine, the mainstay of the town, threw our plans into chaos. The mine was closing. It was unimaginable to the little town. Jobs disappeared overnight. People left. Businesses closed. Schools were reduced to one location and one class. Government offices shut down. Churches closed. Town-folk, who had spent a lifetime working at the mine, simply had to pack their bags and leave on the once-a-week airliner that would soon stop coming. Houses and possessions were left behind. It happened quickly.

It was a disruptive and discouraging time. Our small air service remained busy servicing the villages beyond the town, but the town itself slowly became almost a ghost town. Only about ten percent of the people remained. Abandoned homes froze up that first winter. Pipes shattered and water gushed into streets creating strange frozen formations. A surreal atmosphere settled over the natural beauty of this little isolated corner of the world. What would we do?

"For my thoughts are not your thoughts, neither are your ways my ways," declares the LORD." Isaiah 55:8 (NIV)

God sees the whole picture when we cannot.

It is easy to forget that when we stand on the ground and see a rainbow, we only see half of it. The beautiful arc of color is only a part of the rainbow. Yet when we see a rainbow from the sky it is a full circle.

When you are flying above the clouds and the sun is just right you can get a rare glimpse of the aircraft's shadow encircled by the whole rainbow.

It is a beautiful reminder that God's perspective is greater than ours and He has us encircled, encased in His love, even when we cannot see it.

Still … we were discouraged to say the least. One morning after John had once again thawed out our water line I put in a load of laundry, made a pot of coffee and welcomed a couple of women in who were at my door looking for a bit of company and a few encouraging words. Boxes of books from the library at the church, now closed, lined the back wall of our office. I had a few books on the kitchen table and I gave them to the women to take with them. We talked and prayed together. After a good visit, some tears and hugs they were on their way, encouraged. I closed the door and walked down the hall of our trailer, tears welling up in my eyes and said, "God, who's going to encourage me?"

I heard an audible voice say, "I AM".

Now, I don't know if you would have heard it had you been in that hallway with me that day. But I did. And those words have stuck with me. In my heart of hearts, I knew God was with me. I knew He would sustain us, and we could keep putting one foot in front of the other knowing He would lead the way as we continued to commit our way to Him.

Nothing changed in our circumstances that day. We still didn't know if we too would have to simply pack our bags and leave, counting our losses. But a peace settled me. God's peace came over me and those words, **"I AM"**, became an anchor in my life.

Eventually we had a buyer for our air service and the planes were moved down river. Our third baby was born that year in a barely functioning hospital. He was truly a gift from God in a difficult time! We miraculously retrieved our initial investment and life moved on.

But the **"I AM"** words echoed in my heart, and I took them with me as we went.

When life is full of question marks and uncertainty, we each hold the invitation from God Himself to this place beyond the chaos. This is the place we are called to. This place, the very heart of God, is an amazing mystery we can participate in as we grow to trust Him. In the first verse of the first chapter of the Bible, the creation narrative introduces God using the ancient Hebrew name, Elohim. The meaning is "strong and faithful one". Yet this name in Hebrew is grammatically plural. He is the LORD God of Heaven and Earth, the Trinity.

As the three come together, Father, Son and Holy Spirit, to work on our behalf, loving us with a reliable love beyond understanding, we find the most amazing, secure and safe place to shelter. It is a place where we are known and loved, strengthened and sustained, in spite of what is going on around us. It is the place where "I AM" holds us securely.

This is our rescue. Where our hearts are redeemed from the darkness, where we are empowered supernaturally and where wisdom is revealed.

This is a place to lean into for shelter from the winds. This is our safe place to rest, and refresh, and receive supernatural courage to face the unknowns. This place is a place of trust, a place of calm, a place of security, a place of certainty in who our God is, even in the midst of uncertainty around us. **"Those who know Your name, trust in You".**

"I am with you always..." Matthew 28:20 (NIV)
"He cares for you..." 1 Peter 5:7 (NIV)

And then there is the promise, the incredible promise, that together we will be filled with the fullness of God, overflowing, enabled, equipped, encouraged, encompassed, empowered, through all that He is as our amazing, loving, three-in-one God. He rescues us, redeems us and reveals Himself to us.

It is here that we are fully equipped to be fully alive, with the fullness of God overflowing in us through His reliable love!

We can go there together.

THE HOLY TRINITY

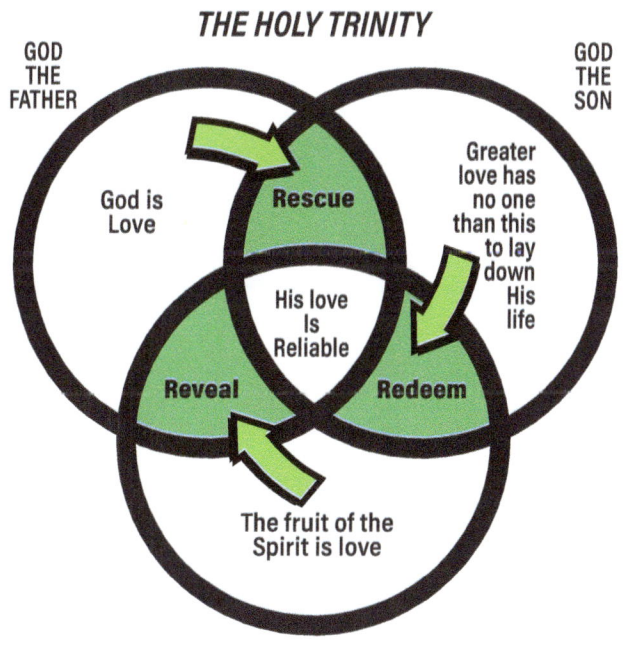

*"I pray that out of his glorious riches
he may strengthen you with power
through his Spirit in your inner being,
so that Christ may dwell in your hearts through faith.*

*And I pray that you, being rooted and established
in love,
may have power,
together with all the Lord's holy people,
to grasp how wide and long and high and deep is the
love of Christ,
and to know this love that surpasses knowledge—
that you may be filled to the measure of all the fullness of God."*
Ephesians 3: 16-19 (NIV)

*May His word steep in our hearts as tea steeps in a pot,
growing stronger as it does.*

PAUSE & PONDER

Consider printing out these verses and memorizing at least the first sentence. Ponder, "Do I truly believe God can strengthen me, through His Holy Spirit so that Jesus Christ, living within me through faith, empowers me, making me fully alive?"

Do I believe His love is reliable? Ask Jesus to help you understand if there is anything that causes you to doubt this love. Invite Him to show you His love for you in a new and fresh way.

Linger here.

Section Four

His reliable love

In the middle of the hard places, it is easy to forget that God has promised to be with us, that He cares for us and about us with a love that is reliable, like no other. In the day-to-day of life sometimes it can feel easy to doubt His love.

When things are not going our way, our natural reaction is often to feel abandoned or to question' God. There were cold days, filled with question marks, when I wondered if we had really been led to that isolated place, as we had believed. Yet without the backdrop of those challenging days, I never would have experienced His voice of comfort as I did that day. I might never have discovered the depth of all that **"I AM"** means in my life.

As the "I AM" voice of years ago kept echoing in my mind and heart, a new picture began to emerge as I studied the names of God the Father, God the Son and God the Holy Spirit. I began to get a glimpse of how the three distinct persons merge and intermingle with one another as One, in the Holy Trinity.

This amazing mystery of God, as three distinct individual persons in the Father, Son and Holy Spirit, yet intertwined as One, inseparable and incredible, is like discovering hidden treasure. The heights and depths are impossible to fathom, yet somehow all a part of the **"I AM"** spoken to me in the hallway of the trailer on that discouraging day years ago.

This mysterious intertwining, **the Trinity,** is the coming together of the very heart of God. This is our secure, very firm place to stand when the winds of uncertainty are howling. This is the place of love that is higher, deeper, wider than we can imagine. This is a love that is reliable, far beyond our understanding.

PAUSE & PONDER

Ponder the love of God. Sit with the thought, "God loves me!"

An old hymn says that if the whole sky were parchment and the oceans were ink, to write the love of God would drain the oceans dry and the scroll of sky could not contain the whole to describe His reliable love. Isn't this a beautiful word picture!

Ask Him now for His help to fully rely on this love, even when, especially when, things are challenging.

> *"And so we know and RELY on the love God has
> for us.
> God is love.
> Whoever lives in love lives in God, and God in him."*
>
> *1 John 4:16 NIV*

We can write it on the tablet of our hearts, making
it personal...
"And so I know and rely on the love God has for me".

God's word reminds us to bookend our day. It reminds us to proclaim God's love in the morning. Before our feet even hit the floor we can pause in thankfulness for this reliable, unending love for us, thanking Him that this love encases us as we head into our day.

Then at night, as our eyes close, we can stop to think about His faithfulness to us throughout the day. Where were His fingerprints? Where did we feel His love? Pondering His faithful love, we can rest peacefully and offer our praise for His faithful presence with us.

"It is good to praise the LORD and make music to your name, O Most High, to proclaim your love in the morning and your faithfulness at night." Psalm 92 :1 & 2 (NIV)

We can create intentional moments in our day to pause and reflect.

PAUSE & PONDER

*Where did I sense the **presence of God the Father** today?*

Where did I see the fingerprint of our majestic, eternal God?

*Where did I feel the **peace of Jesus, God the Son,** today?*

In the quiet as I chose my focus?

In the midst of chaos as I turned to invite Him into the moment?

*Where did I feel the **power of the Holy Spirit** strengthening me today?*

In a moment when I held my tongue?

In the realization that someone in front of me needed to be seen or heard?

Take a moment and offer praise for His love and faithfulness today.

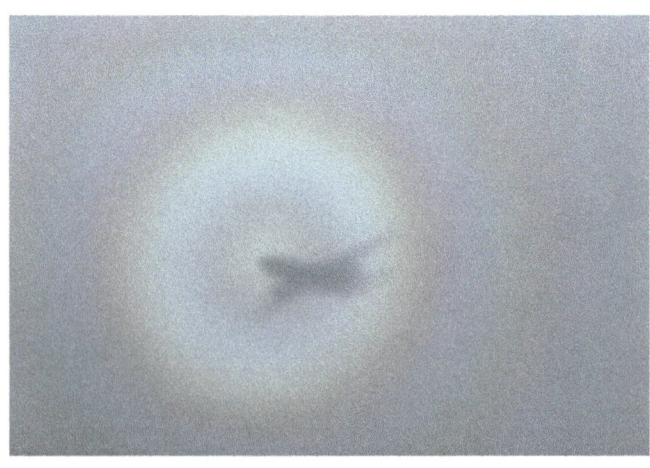

"Where you focus, you follow."

Where we focus is our choice. What we keep front and center becomes our focus.

Just as looking at something in the ditch while driving will unintentionally take us in that direction, so our own daily focus can keep us going forward or steer us off course.

We can choose to focus on God's reliable love in all we encounter today. Pause to take time to think about it.

When things are not going as planned remember His reliable love for you and thank Him that He is present with you in this moment, even when you cannot see the whole picture.

He can rescue, redeem and reveal His ways to us as we trust Him to show us the way. His peace is His gift to us even among the question marks of life as we focus our trust on Him.

Focus on Thanksgiving

Heavenly Father,

As I begin to get a glimpse of You in the fullness of the Trinity, my heart overflows with wonder. Long ago You planned my rescue from the darkness that seeks to over-shadow my mind and heart today. You sent Jesus to buy back my life from the things that wear me down. And after He arose from the grave and ascended again to Heaven, You sent Your Holy Spirit to reveal truth and wisdom to me, to give me discernment. You sent Him to strengthen me with power, in my inner being, from the storehouse of Your glorious riches. Thank you!

Thank you for Your great love that is greater than I could ever imagine. Thank you that as I look at Your names, and Jesus' own declarations of who He is, and as I experience the rich resources of Your Holy Spirit, I get to see a glimpse of You in all Your wonder and majesty.

When my burdens take front and center stage, please help me to lift my eyes off the cares to see Your loving face and know Your presence and peace.

Your holy wholeness is available to move me toward living fully alive in my inner being. Thank you! May my trust in You grow and my confidence in Your steadfast love root me in this firm place to stand. Thank you that I can truly rely on Your love encasing me. I pray this with thanksgiving in the powerful name of Jesus. Amen

"Those who know Your name trust in You.

For You, LORD, have never forsaken

those who seek You."

Psalm 9:10 NIV

His Love is Reliable

Fully loved. Fully Alive!

"And so we know and RELY on the love God has for us".
1 John 4:16 (NIV)

THE HOLY TRINITY

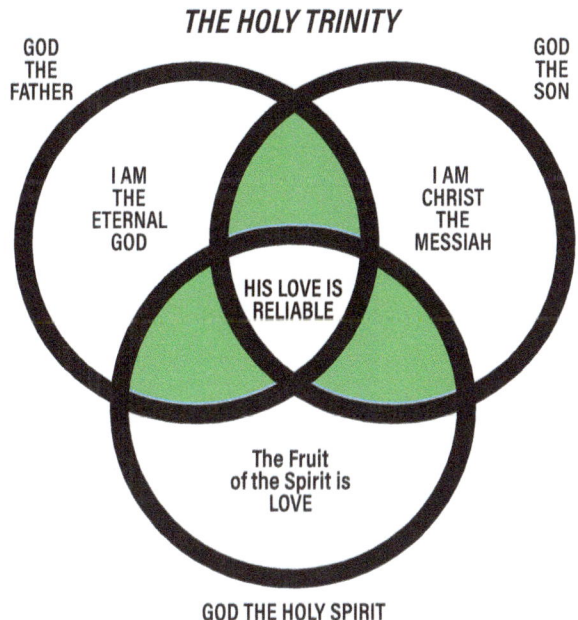

"I pray that out of His glorious riches
He may strengthen you with power
through His Spirit in your inner being,
so that Christ may dwell in your hearts through faith.

And I pray that you, being rooted and established in love,
may have power, together with all the Lord's holy people,
to grasp how wide and long and high and deep is the love of
Christ, and to know this love that surpasses knowledge—
that you may be filled to the measure of all the fullness
of God."
Ephesians 3: 16-19 (NIV)

CHAPTER THREE

THE GREAT EXCHANGE

GOD'S NAMES. GOD'S NATURE. GOD'S PROMISES.

CHAPTER THREE

THE GREAT EXCHANGE

Section One
WHO AM I?

Dust wafted up from the old suitcase as Dad and I unpacked the old pages. Photos, brittle birth certificates and worn-out pages began to make a map of our family history. It was good. It gave me a knowledge of where I came from and who some of my ancestors were. Dad came for the week, and we covered the kitchen table with charts, photos and old documents. As coffee ups were filled regularly, we enjoyed the experience of discovering family traits and resemblances.

Regardless of our individual family histories, as Christians we have a specific heritage. God spells out the family archives for us, so we have a sense of our roots and a knowledge of belonging to the family of faith.

Hebrews chapter 11 lists some of our spiritual ancestors who still inspire us with their faith and remind us of the importance of trusting God.

- Abraham, who heard God say "go" and he went, not knowing his destination.

- Noah, who prepared for a flood while the sun shone and the people laughed.

- Joseph, who trusted his God even when his family deserted him, and he found himself captive in a strange land.

- Moses, who believed God and led the people to the Red Sea where God miraculously parted the waters to make a way where there was no way.

- Joshua, who obeyed the "off the wall" instructions to march around the city of Jericho with lanterns and capture it by faith without a battle.

It is important to recall those who have gone before us, to remember those whose faith in God was strong as He led them. Reading their stories helps us focus on God's faithfulness in who He is. It helps keep our feet firmly planted, less likely to get tangled in distractions.

God will be as faithful to us as He was to our spiritual forefathers as we trust Him. It's good to learn who our trustworthy

God is! Our spiritual family tree archives show us we have a strong heritage!

Figuring out just who we are as individuals is an adventure. Sometimes we see ourselves through the lens of our jobs or our hobbies. Sometimes we find our self-worth in the things we are good at, how we look, what we have or in the good things people say about us.

And sometimes we beat ourselves up and see ourselves negatively or "less than" because of choices we have made or because of the way we may have been treated by others.

Sometimes the family we came from or the place we were born imbeds a negative or a positive picture on our hearts. It is a journey every person takes as we explore who we are and what identity we claim as our own.

The Bible tells us exactly who we are. It is powerful and positive. When we put on the glasses of God's word and see ourselves as God sees us, through the lens of love, it is transformative!

Our identity as believers is wrapped up in who the Father, the Son and the Holy Spirit are, individually and as the mystery of the Three-in-One Trinity. It's an amazing identity we can claim as we trust His character and His love.

When our daughter and I had the opportunity to visit Scotland, I was very interested in the beautiful tartans that represented the various clans throughout the land. Each pattern could be identified with a particular group of families claiming a certain ancestor.

Family crests and family coats-of-arms offer a similar symbolism that represents a certain family, their history or traits, offering an identity over that group of people.

We also have a symbolism of what represents us as believers. When we are baptized into faith in Jesus, these powerful words are spoken over us: "Upon the confession of your faith in Jesus, I baptize you in the name of the Father and of the Son and of the Holy Spirit". We gain a new identity. We have a new lens through which we not only see God, but we see ourselves as well.

Isaiah 61:10 paints a picture of being wrapped in a new robe, clothed in garments of salvation, our old, stained clothes cast aside. Our independent waywardness and self-focused choices, that moved us in a direction away from God, are covered with His righteousness. As we choose to accept His invitation and step into a new identity, His banner of love now symbolizes our identity in the family of God.

"I delight greatly in the LORD; my soul rejoices in my God, for he has clothed me with garments of salvation and arrayed me in a robe of righteousness." Isaiah 61:10 (NIV)

As we glimpse our great God and share our stories of His transformation in our lives, we realize afresh how we are truly changed as we accept this covering of His robe of righteousness. It not only encases us in who He is but transforms our character with the character traits that we see in the LORD our God, as Father, Son and Holy Spirit. The mystery of the Trinity alive in us.

PAUSE & PONDER

Are there titles that I wear on the inside of my heart that whisper things from my past that still try to define me?

Are there choices I have made that still cause remorse or shame? Perhaps it is time to take off those stained garments and give them to God. Ask Jesus, "Am I hanging on to any old and heavy robes of identity that need to go?" What do I hear the Spirit whisper to my heart?

SECTION TWO

GOD THE FATHER - JEHOVAH TSIDKENU

The LORD is our Righteousness!

One of the Hebrew names of God is "Jehovah Tsidkenu", meaning "righteousness" in English. The prophet Jeremiah used it in talking about the LORD Almighty. It is recorded in Jeremiah 23:6 (NIV).

"This is the name by which He shall be called, The LORD Our Righteousness".

Jeremiah was condemning the unfaithful leaders, the "shepherds" who had no spiritual concern for, nor had they protected the people of God, but had carelessly allowed them to be scattered. As a result, God's people were now living in rebellion to Him. Jeremiah was known as the "weeping prophet" because he yearned for his people to be in right relationship with God again. For years he warned the people to turn back to God. He knew the importance of living under God's blessing, and the consequence of turning away.

Jeremiah not only warned the people, but he also prophesied hope to them.

"The days are coming," declares the LORD, "when I will raise up to David a righteous Branch, a King who will reign wisely and do what is just and right in the land. In his days Judah will be saved and Israel will live in safety. This is the name by which he will be called: The LORD Our Righteousness." Jeremiah 23:5,6 (NIV)

Jeremiah was referencing the Almighty God who declared He would fulfill His promise to His people by bringing the righteousness of a Holy God to them, making a way back to blessing and connection with God. This scripture points to the prophetic reference of Jesus when Jeremiah announces that "a righteous branch will come from the ancestry line of David". God's rescue plan for the people He created and loved was in motion. His plan to send Jesus to be "The LORD Our Righteousness", was being prophesied to give the people hope. God would send His righteousness, providing a way to restored relationship and blessing between God and human-kind. He was pointing to the future Messiah, Jesus who would accomplish this provision through His death and resurrection.

To be righteous is not to be self-promoting or performing for applause or praise from others. It is not a parade of our own goodness seeking to showcase our own righteousness. That is what we know as "self-righteous" and it's not pretty. Yet we also know that all of us can also have less than honor-able tendencies that can threaten to derail our lives. The Bible acknowledges this and speaks wisdom when it tells us:

> *"Above all else, guard your heart,*
> *for everything you do flows from it."*
> *Proverbs 4:23 (NIV)*

To know "The LORD Our Righteousness" is to believe that God's love for us, regardless of our performance, is strong and unfailing. He desires to be in relationship with us and to help us guard our hearts. His plan is to pour life into our often-parched souls, so that life-giving words and actions can flow from us to those around us, pointing to His power and His righteousness in our lives.

Yet our own self-reliance and independent spirits often keep God at a distance. Still, God, as the LORD of righteousness, planned a way to bridge the gap between His holiness and our lack of it, so we could enjoy an un-distanced relationship with Him. He planned, out of His great love for us, to cover our inad-equacies and the bent and broken places in our hearts, with

His love and goodness. He planned for our brokenness and our consuming inward self-absorption to be turned outward toward joy.

We all know the desire deep within us for "more". We think it is more of what this world offers. We all know the desire for that one thing that we believe will bring us satisfaction and real purpose in life. It might be some new technology we believe would make life wonderful, or a vacation that tops the charts. It might be getting in shape, landing the dream job, starting a new career, starting a family, winning the lottery, a new home, a new relationship, or just time to pursue the things we love. We all have our own "If only" lists that we believe would bring the ultimate joy.

Yet, we also know how once we do get those desires of our hearts, the joy they bring can tarnish and something new and shiny can soon become our passion and focus. We seek to fill the deep places of our souls with our own resources and that most often finds us coming up short.

This happens to us because the Bible tells us that "God has set eternity in the hearts of humanity..." (Ecclesiastics 3:11 NIV). Only things of eternal, lasting value will truly satisfy us. Really only a relationship with Him, our Creator who knows us better than we know ourselves, will fill the deep empty places in our souls.

God crafted a plan of how we could move from self-focused weariness to truly enjoying His presence and His righteousness. I have found that the missing piece in life, even when we often cannot quite identify what exactly we are seeking, is to be in connection with God who loves us and whom we can trust. I believe it is a deep desire within each of us to be connected to the One who came to bring us life to the full. Not simply "getting by" or "surviving", but truly experiencing what Jesus called "life to the full". (John 10:10 NIV). There are many short-lived counterfeits promising abundant life and peace, yet Jesus is the One who promised a peace that the world cannot give, a "peace which transcends all understanding". (Philippians 4:6 -7 NIV)

God the Father, Jehovah Tsidkenu, planned how He would send a Savior who would be that bridge so we could have peace and be in relationship with Him. As we are covered by His white robe of righteousness, we are freed from the tattered clothing of hurts that harmed us, and from our own heavy marks of guilt and condemnation. As we invite Him into the dark places, He brings His love and light.

God's love points to Jesus, the coming Savior, who would be that bridge to a relationship with Him and to times of refreshing for our souls. When we feel flat and dry, in need of refreshing, it is good to ask ourselves if we have picked up an old garment of something that robs us of peace or brings in weariness from past hurts.

A refocus back to that connection with God can remove and cover over that self-focus and turn our hearts upward to Him and outward to others. As we guard our hearts, He shows us what empty places within us need to be replaced by His righteous covering as He re-robes us in His refreshing.

"The Law of the LORD is perfect, refreshing the soul.
The statutes of the LORD are trustworthy,
making wise the simple." Psalm 19:7 (NIV)

PAUSE & PONDER

Think of yourself with the white robe of righteousness that God offers, covering all the stains and spots and weariness of striving in our own goodness. Thank Him for the cleansing that He alone can bring.

Are there any old garments that are hanging around from your own actions or actions taken against you? Are there things that seek to define you with old words rather than with God's blessing?

Take some time in the quietness of God's presence and offer to Him all those negative words, hurts, disappointments, even anger at oneself or others. Picture yourself before God, receiving His covering over you to transform you with His own righteousness.

Section Three

GOD THE SON

"I AM the Resurrection and the Life"

God the Son, Jesus, came to this earth as a tiny baby. He was fully God, sent from God the Father, yet fully man and human in every way as well. Jesus was perfect because in His human form He stayed closely connected to and communicating with the Father continually.

In so doing, He escaped that self-reliance that keeps us holding God at a distance. (John 5:19,10) In the culture of His day many followed Him as He performed miracles and taught about God. His message was different than that of the message of performance taught in the local places of worship.

Many of the people of that day believed He was the one who would be their rising leader to rescue them politically. But when He didn't and when the crowds turned against Him, His followers were crushed that the one they thought was their Savior was cruelly crucified and laid in a grave. They were shaken, devastated, hopeless.

Yet three days later the most important event in the history of humanity took place.

God raised Jesus from the dead.
All of death and darkness was defeated as Jesus rose to new life.
"I AM the resurrection and the life." John 11:25 (NIV)

All the defeat of the soul, the destruction of joy and the empty state of the inner human being, was conquered. God's plan was that Jesus would take the punishment on Himself for all of mankind's resistance to God, so that each human ever to live would have the opportunity to be in connection with God the Father Himself and receive a new identity in Christ Jesus. Saying "Yes" to this relationship begins the journey of walking with Jesus. Transformation from our inner darkness to His light becomes possible.

Seeing Things Differently

The intriguing story is told in John 11 where Jesus first declared, *"I AM the resurrection and the life"*. Jesus was called to come to the home of his friends, Mary, Martha and Lazarus. The message said Lazarus was sick and they needed Jesus to come. Mary and Martha had seen Jesus heal many times and there was no doubt in their minds that He could and would heal their brother. They were close friends. Jesus often stopped at their home as he traveled to and from Jerusalem.

Yet Jesus lingered in answering the call. When he finally arrived, Lazarus had died. The record states that Martha went out to meet Jesus when she heard He had arrived. But ... it says Mary stayed home.

I can just imagine Mary grieving, not only that her brother was dead, but also that the Lord, who she believed could heal, had not come. Mary was the gentle-spirited sister who would sit at Jesus' feet when He would visit. She loved to be in His presence and listen to His teaching. Even Martha had asked the Lord to rebuke Mary for not helping her as she bustled around the kitchen on one of His visits. Jesus had responded that Mary had chosen the one thing that was most important, that of learning from and being with Jesus.

So, when Mary heard Jesus was coming, she didn't even go out to meet Him. Her devastation and grief must have been overwhelming. As Martha approached Jesus, she was quick to let Him know that, had He been there on time her brother would not have died. Jesus responded to her with the very words, *"I AM the resurrection and the life"*. I'm sure Martha didn't understand the depth of what Jesus was saying. The profound statement would carry even greater understanding a short time later when Jesus Himself would die and be raised to life.

Martha called Mary to come. Mary and the mourners with her all said how surely Jesus could have kept this man from dying had He come sooner. Jesus saw their grief and felt the brokenness of their hearts and He too wept. Then He called for the stone to be removed from the grave even as they objected that the smell would be offensive. The stone was removed, Jesus looked to Heaven and prayed to the Father and then, in a loud voice called out, "Lazarus, come forth!" And the dead man came to life!

We can only imagine the relief, the amazement and the wonder at this miracle! Mary knew Jesus as Healer and when He didn't answer the call as she believed He would she was heartbroken. Yet Jesus delayed, feeling the grief yet desiring to show Himself in a whole new way. Not only would the sisters know Him as Healer but now as the Resurrection and the Life.

This declaration of Jesus, ***"I AM the Resurrection and the Life"*** is still true of Him today. He is the one who can bring life back into the devastated places of our hearts and resurrect healing and hope.

> ***"Therefore, if anyone is in Christ, he is a new creation;***
> ***the old has gone, the new has come!"***
> ***2 Corinthians 5:17 (NIV)***

PAUSE & PONDER

Sometimes we carry hurt or disappointment, even bitterness, feeling that God didn't show up when we believed He would. Invite God into that place of hurt. Ask Him to show Himself to you in a brand-new way. Invite Him to bring new life to the places that have felt lifeless. Linger awhile inviting His resurrection power to bring new life in your soul.

Section Four

GOD THE HOLY SPIRIT

The Spirit of Truth

Connecting with God, through faith in Jesus, positions all who believe to access this internal strength and perseverance. The Spirit of Truth speaks truth into our own hearts gently and wisely. The power of the Holy Spirit is ours to access and to walk transformed through the difficulties of life, through all the things that try to pull our bodies, minds and spirits down to defeat.

This choice, this decision to embrace God's gift of righteousness makes us "a new creation". (2 Corinthians 5:16-21). The only criteria is to speak this truth from one's mouth, that God has raised Jesus from the dead, and believe in one's heart and that person will be "saved". He will be saved to experience eternity in Heaven, saved to be fully alive in his inner being, filled with confident joy and trust in the LORD Himself through all the daily things of life. He will be saved to be transformed by relationship with the LORD God through all the fullness of the Trinity, saved to live free, fully alive!

We find purpose and fulfilment as we become God's child, a reflection of His righteousness here on earth.

What a lens through which to see ourselves! Our old selves are covered, cleansed, wrapped in robes of righteousness. (Isaiah 61:10). Truly "new creations", dressed differently than we were, with new purpose and tasks to fulfill us.

"For we are God's workmanship, created in Christ Jesus to do good works, which God prepared in advance for us to do."
Ephesians 2:10 (NIV)

"We are therefore Christ's ambassadors...so that in him we might become the righteousness of God".
2 Corinthians 5:17-21 (NIV)

Some of those who believe seem content to know their place in heaven is secured by their belief. They may participate in the organization of "church", yet the fulfillment and purposes of Christ in their lives often feels distant. There may even be a longing for the "more" to be fulfilled through the things this world offers with the fleeting promise of joy. That is where the often neglected third person of the Trinity is needed, God the Holy Spirit.

God the Holy Spirit was sent after Jesus ascended back to Heaven following His great resurrection. (John 16:7) The Spirit was sent to indwell every believer in Jesus! What a thought that is! (1 Corinthians 3:16 & 6:19).

We can believe and receive. This is so profoundly simple yet, so simply profound!

"That you might be filled to the measure of all the fullness of God!" Ephesians 3:19 (NIV)

When we are baptized into faith in Jesus and "in the name of the Father, Son and Holy Spirit", we often have little grasp of the enormity of this declaration.

In the early days of the church, believing and baptism went hand in hand. When one says "yes" to stepping into the new life Jesus offers and a step of faith is taken to believe, it makes complete sense that baptism follows quickly. Saying "Yes" to following Jesus in baptism is our outward symbol to the world. Saying "Yes" to the infilling of the Spirit of God is our inward invitation, not just to a restored relationship with God, but to the transforming power of the Spirit within us! The power-house of the indwelling Holy Spirit comes in fullness. It is a deep commitment to a brand-new identity. It is access!

This is our hope, our confident expectation of the glory and presence of God in our lives through the Holy Spirit! It is peace with God, the one thing our hearts crave.

"Through Christ we have gained access by faith into this grace in which we now stand. And we rejoice in the hope of the glory of God."
Romans 5:2 (NIV)

What a cause we have for rejoicing!

We now have a secure place where we can access God's power to transform our inner beings. We have a place where we can exchange our insufficiencies for His sufficiency.

We often try to hide our inadequacies, yet God tells us these are the very entry points for His power in our lives. These are the very points where we can experience His transforming power.

"The Lord said to me, "My grace is sufficient for you, for my power is made perfect in weakness." Therefore, I will boast all the more gladly about my weaknesses, so that Christ's power may rest on me." 2 Corinthians 12:9 (NIV)

This is the Great Exchange!

The Great Exchange is our heritage as believers in Jesus. It is our place of belonging because He is Jehovah Tsidkenu, our righteousness, our covering, our empowerment by His Spirit, His resemblance in us!

- *Exchanging my powerless footing for His powerful position.* This is the place where we have gained access to His grace. (Romans 5:1,2).

- *Exchanging my weariness for His refreshment.* It is a place to upload our burdens and our cares, our desires and our needs through time spent releasing to Him the things that keep us awake at night, trusting Him to manage the outcome. (Matthew 11:28) (1 Peter 5:7)

- *Exchanging my lack for His abundance.* It is a place to download all the resources of the Holy Spirit. He offers all the strength we need to cultivate His fruit of love, joy, peace, patience, kindness, goodness, faithfulness, gentleness and self-control. These can be ours by simply acknowledging where we are weak and inviting Him into that place, that relationship, that circumstance. As we release our cares to Him, He releases His power in us to walk in His strength. (Galatians 5:22 NIV)

- It can be helpful to choose one of the nine fruits of the Spirit that we would like more of in our hearts and invite the Holy Spirit to be at work in us to produce it. The results will amaze you.

- *Exchanging my old behaviors for His character traits in my life.* The Great Exchange is our place to throw off the old garments of guilt and shame that we so easily pick up. We have access to His grace and His love to put on the "spiritual wardrobe" we need to live and walk in our daily lives clothed with His character. (Galatians 3:27). He empowers us to put on His love and grace and strength, fresh and new every day as we need it, ask for it and receive it.

- *Exchanging my judgment of others for the tender compassion and love of Christ.* We have a place to put off the old and hardened places of our hearts and put on new attitudes of love and kindness, gentleness and humility. (Colossians 3). We can truly exchange our harsh judgments for His loving care. He works in us to make these changes and this fruit is visible. As we recognize the hardness within us, we can invite Him to soften our attitudes and give us His wisdom.

- ***Exchanging my overwhelming trouble for His strength to overcome.*** We have a place where our identity is reflected back to us through the lens of all Christ is in us, and we experience ourselves empowered by the Spirit of God as an overcomer and no longer a victim of the darkness. (John 16:33).

- ***Exchanging my helplessness for the authority and power of Christ.*** We have a place to access and put on the "full armor of God" so that we can stand strong against the darkness that seeks to pull us down. (Ephesians 6)

In the Father, the Son and the Holy Spirit we are given access to a very deep place, a firm place to stand and not be shaken, even in shaking times. We have access through our belief in Jesus and the power of the Spirit! We exchange our old nature for His divine nature, an anchor that holds us firmly even when clouds gather and winds of uncertainty blow.

> *"We have this hope as an anchor for the soul, firm and secure."*
> *Hebrews 6:19 (NIV)*

Linger over these promises from God...

"The fruit of the Spirit is love, joy, peace, patience, kindness, goodness, faithfulness, gentleness and self-control ... Since we live by the Spirit, let us keep in step with the Spirit."

Galatians 5:22-25 (NIV)

"And God is able to make all grace abound to you, so that in all things at all times, having all that you need, you will abound in every good work." 2 Corinthians 9:8 (NIV)

PAUSE & PONDER

"The old has gone. The new is here."

Christ in you is your hope!

Whenever you recognize an attitude, behavior, word, that represents negativity, a tearing down rather than building up, or a helplessness that feels overwhelming, PAUSE. Recognize that you have taken an old garment out of your mental clothes closet, one that no longer represents who you are because of Jesus.

These no longer serve us, as believers in Jesus, nor do they serve the people and situations around us.

We have access to a place in Christ Jesus to exchange the old for something new. He offers new fruit to grow in our lives.

Simply ask, in the moment, for the help of the Holy Spirit.

"LORD God, I am out of _____(patience, hope, peace, name whatever it is you need.) Please exchange my_____(impatience, hopelessness, anxiety, name your weakness) for Your strength in this moment by the power of Your Holy Spirit. Amen."

"May grace and perfect peace cascade over you
as you live in the rich knowledge of God and of Jesus
our Lord.

Everything we could ever need for life and godliness
has already been deposited in us by His divine power.

For all this was lavished upon us through the rich experi-
ence of knowing Him
who called us by name and invited us to come to Him
through a glorious manifestation of His goodness.
As a result of this, He has given you magnificent promises
that are beyond all price,
so that through the power of these tremendous promises
we can experience partnership with the divine nature,
by which you have escaped the corrupt desires that are of
the world."
2 Peter 1, 3 & 4 TPT

PAUSE & PONDER

Holy Father,

I give You thanks for covering me with Your righteousness. All my spots and blemishes of selfishness and self-interest get covered with the white robe of righteousness that You put on me when I declared my faith in Jesus.

Forgive me for the times I get re-focused on what You have covered. Thank you that Your word says You remove our trespasses as far as the East is from the West. Forgive my feeble attempts to be righteous in my own strength.

Thank you that You are the LORD who is mighty to save me. Thank You that you rescue circumstances and situations that need Your redemption. May I give up my own attempts to control the outcomes. May I rest today and simply follow Your lead.

You alone are the Righteous One. Christ alone brings new life.

Your Spirit is the One who alone can bring truth, strength, righteousness and hope to my life.

Thank you for Your saving grace and abundant love that brings Your Fountain of Living water to my life. Help me to walk today in that refreshing and the joy of Your covering of righteousness over me. May I seek to know You in Your fullness, with my whole heart, exchanging my weaknesses for Your strength. In the powerful name of Jesus', I pray. Amen.

He Transforms Me

The Father gives His covering.
The Son brings new life.
The Spirit transforms me.

THE GREAT EXCHANGE

THE HOLY TRINITY

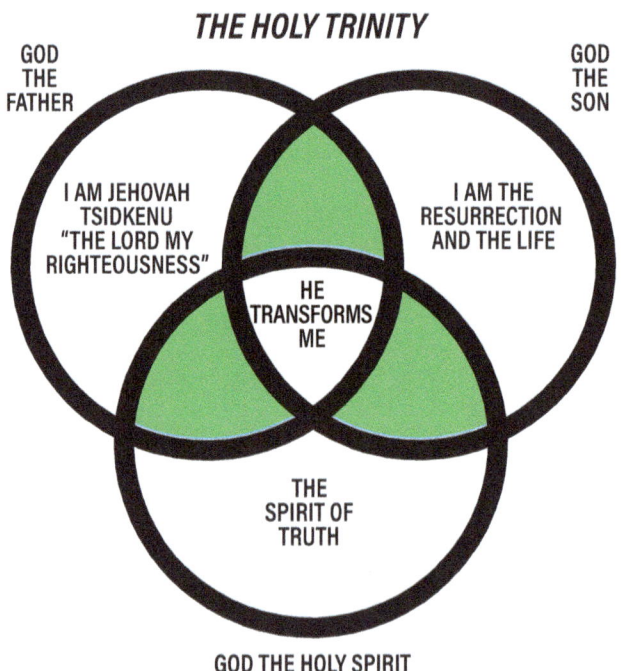

GOD THE FATHER

GOD THE SON

I AM JEHOVAH TSIDKENU "THE LORD MY RIGHTEOUSNESS"

I AM THE RESURRECTION AND THE LIFE

HE TRANSFORMS ME

THE SPIRIT OF TRUTH

GOD THE HOLY SPIRIT

"His divine power has given us everything we need for life and godliness through our knowledge of Him."
2 Peter 1:3

The Holy Spirit transforms me.

CHAPTER FOUR

NEVER ALONE

GOD'S NAMES. GOD'S NATURE. GOD'S PROMISES.

CHAPTER FOUR

JEHOVAH SHAMMAH

The LORD is there

Section One

The log in the fireplace had grown cold. It had rolled away from the center where the other logs were burning brightly as they shared the flame. It is a great picture of what isolation does to our souls. We were created to be in relationship. Our hearts desire a connectedness, a fellowship, a place where we are not alone.

Ruth's Story

Ruth, my mom, had walked with the LORD for all her adult life. In her late teens she came face-to-face with death when she was in a car/train accident. It took the life of her friend. Her own coat tail was severed on the rails as the train sped by. She was badly injured. As she felt her insides sloshing, she had asked God to save her life, and He did.

Years later, after decades of walking connected to God and His word, fully assured of His presence with her and fully trusting Him, Ruth found herself isolated in a senior's home. The flu was rampant and several of the residents were confined to their rooms while nurses in isolation garb made their rounds as short as possible. I talked to Mom daily on the phone. She was in good spirits and other than a mild case of the flu she was just fine. She reassured me, "I'm not alone. Jesus is here with me." Other residents didn't fare as well, and some were deeply agitated at being isolated.

The presence of the LORD made all the difference for Ruth. "The LORD is there", was our comfort as we looked at her circumstance. God was with Ruth as she navigated her quiet days. She enjoyed a companionship, a fellowship with the Holy Spirit that made all the difference.

Most of us can recall times when we have been lonely; lonely in a room full of people, lonely at church or even when out and about seeing others enjoying one another's company. Loneliness can sneak up on us after a move, a death of a loved one, a loss of various kinds and, if we aren't careful, loneliness can draw us into isolation.

God addresses loneliness as well. Even the Trinity, our three-in-one God signifies community.

Hebrews 13:5 (NIV) assures us of the deep value of God's presence, "**Keep your lives free from the love of money and be content with what you have, because God has said, "Never will I leave you; never will I forsake you."**

We recall the prophecy in Isaiah of Jesus' coming and the repeat of that message in Matthew's record of Jesus birth where His very name means "God with us". "**All this took place to fulfill what the Lord had said through the prophet: "The virgin will conceive and give birth to a son, and they will call him Immanuel" (which means "God with us")." Matthew 1:22-23 (NIV)**

Jesus Himself, after His resurrection and before He left this earth to return to Heaven, spoke these comforting words to those who follow Him, "**And surely, I AM with you always, to the very end of the age." Matthew 28:20 (NIV)**

He further stated that the Holy Spirit would be sent, after His resurrection and return to Heaven, and that this Spirit of Truth would be with us and in us, forever. ***"And I will ask the Father, and he will give you another Advocate to help you and be with you forever - the Spirit of Truth. The world cannot accept him, because it neither sees him nor knows him. But you know him, for he lives with you and will be in you." John 14:16-17 (NIV)***

A story is told of a bag lady who died in poverty only to have her true identity discovered after her death. It was said that she was the missing daughter of a wealthy family. Not knowing the rich inheritance that was hers, she lived a lonely life of isolation and deprivation.

Whether the story is true or not, it does make one realize that we too can go through life unaware of the rich inheritance God offers us. We need not live in isolation nor poverty of spirit when our loving God offers us the opportunity to be encased by the Father, Son and Holy Spirit forever. We need only to bring our brokenness to Him.

SECTION TWO

GOD THE FATHER - JEHOVAH SHAMMAH

The Lord is there

The Jewish priest, Ezekiel, was taken captive to Babylon along with thousands of other Jews. The story is recorded in the Bible in the book bearing his name. The Jews had rebelled against God and had turned to depending on their own strengths and the political strength of other nations. Ezekiel was also a prophet of God. He warned the people of their independent spirit and urged them to turn back to God. They ignored Ezekiel's warnings. Because of their self-dependence that ignored God, God withdrew His presence, His glory. It was a dark time for the Israelites. It seemed a pattern for them since their miraculous escape from Egypt led by Moses through the Red Sea. They trusted. They doubted. They rebelled against God. They choose to lean on their own understanding of life with no thought of God. They suffered the consequence. Yet God never stopped seeking them.

It is a good reminder to keep our own hearts checked for that independence from God. It can slip in so easily as we rely on our own understanding of things. It bears its own consequences as well.

Ezekiel could have easily slipped into rebellion against God too, along with the others. He also found himself captive in a strange land where his voice was not heard, even by his own people. But during this time of disorientation and confusion he kept his focus. God spoke to Ezekiel and showed him a vision of hope for the people. Even in spite of hardened hearts toward Him, God's amazing love desired to bring a message of hope to His people.

God was showing Ezekiel that He still cared and that He was there with His people even when they did not acknowledge Him.

God showed Ezekiel a vision of a valley full of very dry bones, bones that God would breathe into and bring life to. When circumstances seemed to have no hope in them, God was giving hope that He would, once again, breathe life into His people. God instructed Ezekiel what to tell the people. He said, *"My dwelling place will be with them; I will be their God, and they will be my people". Ezekiel 37:27 (NIV)*

Even in the midst of hardened hearts toward Him, God desired to reach His people with hope. He wanted them to know that He would again restore Jerusalem, for their hearts were broken at its destruction. Ezekiel went on to prophesy that a time would come when God would rebuild His temple, calling it **Jehovah Shammah, "The LORD is there".**

The word "hope" in the Hebrew language of the Old Testament means "waiting" and "waiting on God". It is a picture of patience, a picture of expectation and encouragement.

This incredible vision was also pointing toward future events. It was again a foreshadowing of a time when God would send Jesus to be our Savior, the one who would redeem us and buy back our brittle and broken pieces. Our own spiritual dry bones would be brought to new life. Jesus would bring restoration to dry souls.

Because God is always present, everywhere, all the time, His omnipresence carries the truth of His name, **God the Father, Jehovah Shammah,** meaning "The LORD is there". He is there in the past, speaking through Ezekiel. He is there, pointing to the coming of Jesus and to the future when believers will be united with Him in Heaven. And He is there, in the present as He was with Ruth. And He is there with you, with us, right where we walk today. The LORD is with me!

God spoke through His prophets in the Old Testament. He told them what to watch for as they awaited rescue and restoration in their various situations. He kept pointing to a coming Savior.

The prophets' visions and words brought hope to the people during the four hundred years of silence between the Old and New testaments. God had made a covenant with Abraham, promising him land, descendants, blessing and redemption. Yet, even in spite of God's presence and His miracles along the way, the hearts of the people became cold and weary of waiting. They turned to idols that replaced God in their lives. Though God's presence and glory withdrew as the people turned away from Him, His love did not. Because of His great love for His people, God kept speaking hope through His prophets. The prophets kept bringing the hopeful message that God had a plan to reconcile His people back to Himself and back to life. He told them just what to watch for, the birth of a baby.

"Therefore, the Lord himself will give you a sign: The virgin will be with child and will give birth to a son, and will call him Immanuel." Isaiah 7:14 (NIV)

Years later, in Matthew chapter one, when the prophecy was again speaking hope to a new generation, the hope-filled name "Immanuel" was highlighted with the knowledge that it meant *God would be with them* through the birth of this coming baby.

Matthew continues with more detail. An angel had instructed a young man named Joseph, to enter freely into marriage with a young woman named Mary. Both Mary and Joseph had visits from angels confirming to them individually that Mary would give birth to a special baby, the Son of God! Both of these young people believed the messages from God and Joseph took Mary as his wife, knowing she was pregnant. This was a courageous step for both of them in the culture of that day. The angel's message to Joseph was profound, *"She will give birth to a son, and you are to give him the name Jesus, because he will save his people from their sins." Matthew 1:21 (NIV)*

What faith these young people had! What risk they were willing to take!

Immanuel, in Hebrew means "God is with us". Jesus, in Hebrew means "The Lord is Salvation". God sent Jesus to be our Salvation, to be there, to be here, to reconcile us and the world to Himself so that we would never need to walk alone again.

PAUSE & PONDER

When we feel alone it can be easy to feel that God has abandoned us.

Sometimes He is waiting for us to abandon our independence from Him and invite Him back into our lives and our specific situations to bring His hope once again.

When the tempting question is, "Why, LORD?", it is sometimes good to ask Him, "What dry bones might You want to bring to life again in my heart, LORD?" Thank you that You are here with me now.

SECTION THREE

GOD THE SON

I AM the Door

God the Son, Jesus Himself, declared *"I am the door; if anyone enters through Me, he will be saved, and will go in and out and find pasture." John 10:9 (NASB)*

Jesus is the open door for us to go through to come into that connection and reconciliation with God. He was called a Man of sorrows and acquainted with grief. He understands the brokenness we experience in this fallen world of dry bones.

The door is open for us to be reconciled in friendship with God through Jesus' sacrifice on the cross. He is "God with us", here, now, today, "with us". He will walk with us. When we invite Him, He resides within us to transform us and to never leave us.

He is also "the God who is there", in the future, not only at the end of our lives on earth, but also at the end of time, ready to receive His own.

"I am the door". The way to God is opened to us by Jesus.

The Message version of the Bible expresses it beautifully in Romans 5:1-5.

"By entering through faith into what God has always wanted to do for us—set us right with Him, make us fit for Him—we have it all together with God because of our Master Jesus.

"And that's not all: We throw open our doors to God and discover at the same moment that He has already thrown open His door to us. We find ourselves standing where we always hoped we might stand—out in the wide-open spaces of God's grace and glory, standing tall and shouting our praise.

"There's more to come: We continue to shout our praise even when we're hemmed in with troubles, because we know how troubles can develop passionate patience in us, and how that patience in turn forges the tempered steel of virtue, keeping us alert for whatever God will do next.

"In alert expectancy such as this, we're never left feeling shortchanged. Quite the contrary—we can't round up enough containers to hold everything God generously pours into our lives through the Holy Spirit!"

Romans 5:1-5 (The Message)

SECTION FOUR

GOD THE HOLY SPIRIT

The Spirit of Understanding

The wind of the Holy Spirit, or the breath of the Spirit, was given as Jesus had promised it would after His resurrection and return to Heaven. This is known as Pentecost. The disciples waited, prayed and expected this gift Jesus had told them would come. He promised this Helper, Comforter and Advocate to be His breath within us.

The breath of God enters us at our physical birth as every baby takes that first breath. The breath of the Spirit enters us as we take that first breath of spiritual life, saying "yes" to Jesus.

This gift of the Holy Spirit, **God the Holy Spirit,** enters us as we profess Jesus as our Savior. But it comes in fullness, filling us with expectation of strength and life and hope as we lean into God's word and experience God's presence daily, saying, "Lord, I am coming".

> *"The mind governed by the flesh is death (dry bones) but the mind governed by the Spirit is life and peace."*
> *Romans 8:6 (NIV)*

When we set our minds on the Spirit there is life and peace. Setting our minds on what our own selfish nature desires brings us into the valley of dry bones. At first it is not that noticeable, but it does not take long to sense the "lack of life".

> ### *PAUSE AND PONDER*
>
> *Where am I camping in my thoughts these days? Is it on dry bones which leave me feeling lifeless and flat, or on the Spirit of God within me inviting me through the door to His peace and life in my heart and mind? Jesus is offering His open door to invite you into His presence as you invite the Holy Spirit to bring life into your mind and heart.*

When the Holy Spirit is invited to come in fullness in our lives, He fills us with divine boldness. (Acts 4:31) Our eyes are opened to His strength and power, to His counsel and wisdom. God reminds us that envy and strife cause confusion, and where there is confusion there is every evil thing. (James 3:16). Confusion is also a door. Where we set our mind opens and closes doors in our lives. When we open the door to Jesus Christ in our lives, there comes knowledge of the Holy, and there is understanding only the Spirit can give. He gives His wisdom and understanding to us. It is the door to His presence and to His peace.

Daily we get to choose the door we want to walk through. It can be either the door of hope and trust and confident expectation, or the door of confusion and wrestling with others in strife. We choose our focus every day.

Where we focus, we follow.

Driving home one dark night I saw a mound in the ditch as my headlights picked it up. Straining to see what was there, I suddenly found myself heading toward the ditch as I focused on what was off the road. I quickly corrected, realizing how easy it is to find ourselves in the ditch when our focus gets distracted.

Sometimes we can feel weary like the people had in Ezekiel's day. We can feel the Lord is long in coming to rescue us as we hoped He would. Instead of patient and hopeful waiting in trust, we can choose "idols" to console us, things that bring only temporary pleasure or relief as the Israelites did, resulting in confusion.

Or we can look at the seemingly impossible road ahead with trust in God, as Joseph did. Genesis 20 records his story of being sold into slavery by his brothers. Yet he trusted God and said, "What others had meant for harm, God used for good", resulting in His peace.

SECTION FIVE

Wide Open Spaces

Both Ezekiel and Joseph chose trusting and walking closely with God in spite of how things looked around them. Ezekiel listened and walked bravely in captivity, foretelling the future judgment, but also the future hope that God revealed through visions. Joseph believed God, listening to his dreams and the words of angels, trusting God to lead him through years of trials, bringing good out of hardship.

Today we have the Holy Spirit to guide us as we enter the door of hope through Jesus. We can ask daily for the Holy Spirit to give us the Spirit of Understanding, and to fill us with awe at who He is in us. (Isaiah 11:1-3)

As we tackle any challenge we face, we can be assured that God is there! God is here! God is with us! God is at work in us and through us!

As we believe in God and rely on Him to walk with us daily, He can be trusted to be there and to empower us by His Spirit through all our days.

The banner of His name is over our burdens. God is there!

Some years ago, I knew a man who had a huge work assignment to complete a task that no one had seemed able to find the way through. He took it on, inviting the Holy Spirit into the assignment and asking for wisdom and insight. He came up with a solution that was applauded.

I too have experienced divine help on projects that simply felt too big for me, and I called on God's help. I am reminded that God places us in positions and situations to show who He is as He works in and through us.

In another intriguing story of Daniel and his three friends who were captive in a strange land, we read in the book of Daniel, *"To these four young men God gave knowledge and understanding of all kinds of literature and learning. And Daniel could understand visions and dreams of all kinds." Daniel 1:17 (NIV)*

God the Father, God the Son, and God the Holy Spirit together as three in One provide a deep, strong and secure place from which we can live because God is there, God is here, and God works in us!

As we throw open our door to God, we discover at the same moment that He has already thrown open His door to us.

These verses from The Message are worth repeating...

"By entering through faith into what God has always wanted to do for us—set us right with Him, make us fit for Him—we have it all together with God because of our Master Jesus.

And that's not all: We throw open our doors to God and discover at the same moment that He has already thrown open His door to us.

We find ourselves standing where we always hoped we might stand—out in the wide-open spaces of God's grace and glory, standing tall and shouting our praise." Romans 5:1 & 2 (The Message)

There is another very practical verse that can help us live our lives in these wide-open spaces even on a "Monday morning".

"Trust in the LORD with all your heart and lean not on your own understanding; in all your ways acknowledge him, and he will make your paths straight." Proverbs 3:5 & 6 (NIV)

When I think of trusting God and acknowledging Him as I walk out my week, I wonder, "What does it look like to acknowledge God in all my ways?" I picture two people coming to a doorway at the same time. One waves his hand and, acknowledging the other gestures, "You go first".

In the same way we can invite God, in all His fullness, to go first into those situations, conversations, meetings, relationships, mealtimes, and into whatever doorways we find ourselves. We invite Him to bring His understanding and wisdom. We can watch Him work on our behalf and for His glory. The results will be surprising, because He is with us. We need not navigate the maze alone.

Because of His promise, *"I am with you always, even unto the end of the world",* we can trust Him every step of the way, for He Himself has said, *"Never will I leave you; never will I forsake you."* Matthew 28:20b (NIV) & Hebrews 13:5 (NIV)

PAUSE AND PONDER

Think about your week and consciously acknowledge God in one situation or relationship by inviting Him to go first into that circumstance this week. Acknowledge His presence there with you. As we relinquish our own understanding of things and open the door to Jesus, trusting Him to work in the moment, His Holy Spirit brings His grace and His wisdom that we can count on.

Music washes the dust off our souls as we tune in to songs of praise to God. Choose to let the words of a song become your prayer today. He is with you.

PAUSE AND PONDER

When could you take time to listen to a few worship songs and ask the Lord what He wants to say to your heart personally? Perhaps on a commute, a walk or a run or just enjoying some stillness without a screen in front of you? Use the words of the songs as prayer prompts from your heart. Pause in His presence to hear His whisper.

SECTION SIX
MAKING IT PRACTICAL
Release. Resist. Rejoice.

Release: When we recognize tension rising within us during the day or night, we can pause and release the source of tension to God. This loosens our grip on it, whether it be anger or frustration, the news that worries, or the irritation of someone's words or actions. Whatever is causing tension to tighten within you, RELEASE it to God specifically and ask Him to calm your heart and mind. He is with you. Ask for His understanding and receive His peace.

Resist: The enemy of our souls will try to reinforce the angst and even tempt us toward isolation. Stand firm against the urge to let the thing fester in your mind, robbing your peace. You are not left alone to handle this on your own. He is with you.

Rejoice: We can remind ourselves of the qualities of Jehovah Shammah, "the God who is there", in whatever is troubling us, reminding ourselves of the door of peace Jesus offers as He is present with us. This changes the focus to thanksgiving for who He is with us in the middle of the concerns.

Rejoice in the fact that the Holy Spirit will give you a spirit of understanding to know Him more through this. Commit to trust God with your whole heart, through this whole thing that troubles you. He is with you.

A PRAYER TO PRAY AS YOUR OWN

Father God,

Thank you that You are the One who watches over me and sees every step I take. Thank you that You are the God who is there in every situation I encounter. You are also the God who is here, walking with me, closer than my own breath. You speak to me, and You hear me when I call.

Thank you, LORD God, that You listen to my heart, and You see the depth of my soul. Nothing of me is hidden from You. You answer before I even call. You know my needs even when I can't find words and before they even reach my prayers. Thank you.

You take delight in me. You desire to have fellowship with me. You, the LORD GOD, the GOD of Heaven, know my name and the place where I live. You know the bed where I lay my head at night. You call me Your own. You actually rejoice over me. Forgive me for the times I take Your presence for granted and rush past You without a nod.

May I bask in Your welcome today and in the warmth of Your love. May it spur me on to be faithful to You, as You are so faithful to me. The Lord is with me, there, here, always, right in each moment. What a treasure that is, LORD! Thank you! I pray this in the strong name of Jesus. Amen.

Never Alone!

"The LORD is a refuge for the oppressed,
a stronghold in times of trouble.
"Those who know your name will trust in you,
for you, LORD, have never forsaken those who seek You."
Psalm 9:9 & 10 (NIV)

Jehovah Shammah
The LORD is there
I am never alone!

THE HOLY TRINITY

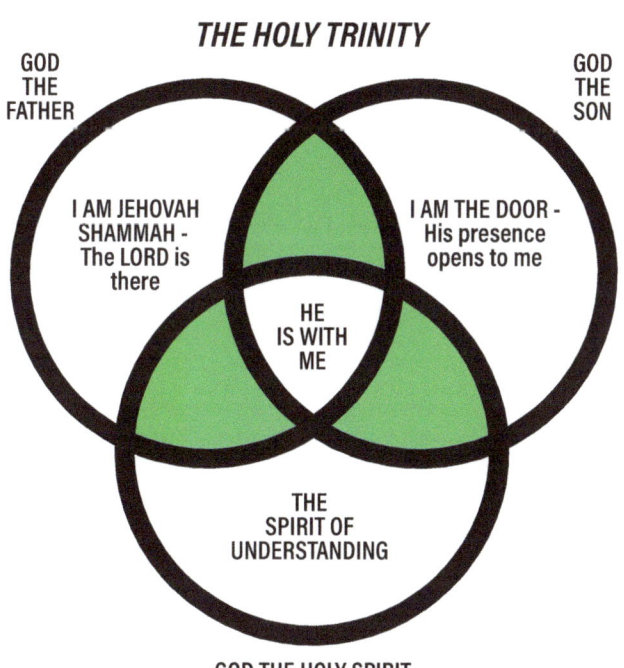

He is with me

"Trust in the LORD with all your heart and lean not on your own understanding; in all your ways acknowledge him, and he will make your paths straight."

Proverbs 3:5 & 6 (NIV)

His presence never leaves me.

CHAPTER FIVE

A WELL-WATERED GARDEN

GOD'S NAMES. GOD'S NATURE. GOD'S PROMISES.

CHAPTER FIVE

JEHOVAH RAAH (ROHI)
The Lord My Shepherd

Section One
A Place of Springs

Nancy was a dear friend of mine for about 20 years. For many of those years Nancy travelled a journey through the valley of cancer. As anyone familiar with that road knows, it is a complicated and difficult journey. The same was true for Nancy. Yet Nancy brought such delight to each of our visits as she chatted easily about the special nearness of Jesus. She knew His presence in a tangible way. His peace radiated from her. Friends and I would regularly go to visit Nancy to encourage her, yet we were the ones who always came away encouraged.

I remember one spring day when a friend and I planted Nancy's flowers while she sat on the front steps chatting with us, too exhausted to participate. She had her usual plate of snacks ready for us, always complete with sweet figs and nuts. Though we insisted she not prepare at all, she always did. Other times another friend and I would sit with Nancy in her sunroom. We'd visit and pray and eat figs together. It might take Nancy most of her morning to prepare that plate, between rests, but it was her loving gesture. The presence of the LORD in that place brought such sweet peace. Visiting

Nancy was a special joy. She knew her Father God, her very close friend, Jesus and the sweet fellowship of the Holy Spirit enabling her in so many ways. She took full advantage of that firm place He offered her. She invited Him into every detail of her day. He guided her and sustained her and walked every step of her journey with her. I was amazed and touched deeply by the presence of God through Nancy.

Nancy honored her LORD. She leaned hard on Him for strength. He gave her joy as they walked closely together. He truly was a tender Shepherd to His beloved lamb. One night Jesus stepped into Nancy's room and took her hand, quietly taking her home with Him. I can only imagine her joy!

I still miss Nancy. She is still remembered in conversations with those two friends with whom I ate figs at Nancy's, years ago. Figs too, always bring her memory back with a smile.

I came across a verse in the Psalms after Nancy went to be with Jesus. I wrote her name in the margin of my Bible beside it.

"As they pass through the Valley of Weeping,
they make it a place of springs; ..."
Psalm 84:6 (NIV)

Even in the valley when things were very hard, Nancy was carried in a way that was remarkable, inspiring and completely supernatural. She rested on Him and in His strength and He truly shepherded her heart. She could make the valley a place of springs, because Nancy knew her God!

> ## PAUSE & PONDER
>
> *Ask the LORD to remind you of a time when His presence comforted or guided you. Perhaps there was a time when you knew it was His hand that rescued you. Stop and thank Him for His tender care to you. Thank Him that His Shepherd heart toward you always desires to guide and protect your heart.*

On our visit to Scotland, my daughter and I saw dozens of sheep on the hillsides. Every flock had a specifically colored spot of paint on each sheep's hip to identify which shepherd or farm it belonged to. Sheep have a tendency to stray. As I learned about them, I found that they are curious, yet fearful. They are afraid of being alone and get stressed when they are. It is easy for a curious or careless sheep to turn aside and get lost. They have great peripheral vision with their eyes set on the sides of their heads and they see best with heads down while grazing. But their eyesight has little depth perception, and they can find themselves down a cliff or caught in brambles before they know it. The shepherd knows his sheep and sees when one is missing and goes to find it. Sheep recognize their shepherd's voice as he comes to rescue them.

Section Two
God the Father - Jehovah Raah
The LORD my Shepherd

In the Old Testament, **God the Father** refers to Himself as a Shepherd for His sheep. In Ezekiel 34 the leaders of the "flock of Israel" had, once again been self-serving, caring more for themselves than for the people. Through the prophet, Ezekiel, God expressed His displeasure at how the flock had been left to be prey as the leaders had discharged their trust of care. The "flock" had scattered, to their own peril.

Through the prophet, God declares, *"I myself will be the Shepherd of my sheep and cause them to lie down in peace, says the Lord God." Ezekiel 34:15 (TLB)*

Another prophet, Isaiah, references the flock this way: ***"All we like sheep have gone astray; we have turned, everyone, to his own way...". Isaiah 53:6 (NKJV)***

When we quit "grazing", that is, taking in God's word, our own vision becomes hampered, just as when the sheep looks to the things that not only spark his curiosity, but also his fears. We can find ourselves alone and stressed as we focus on the things swirling around us. Our own depth perception in life becomes limited as we tend to focus on the distracting or fearful things around us. We can find ourselves down a slippery slope, caught up in brambles too.

From time-to-time we all have areas in our lives where it can be hard to acknowledge what is happening in our own hearts and minds. It can be easier to turn to busyness, constant background noise or zoning out on screens to occupy our minds rather than looking inward to what our hearts long for.

Tuning in to the distractions and fears can leave us feeling vulnerable, even caught in a snare, whether of our own making or that of others. Our perceptions become clouded, and we can find ourselves feeling lost, flat, adrift or astray, turning to our own ways to seek our own solutions.

The reading in Isaiah continues and Isaiah makes a bold proclamation, ***"All we like sheep have gone astray and we have turned, everyone, to his own way... and the LORD has laid on Him the iniquity of us all." Isaiah 53:6 (NKJV)***

Isaiah the prophet was pointing to the future Jesus, the LORD, who would come to this earth and redeem every lost wanderer who asks. Because of God's great love for us His Shepherd's heart was to rescue us, each and every one of us, from the brambles we find ourselves snared in, due to our own short sightedness.

Psalm 23 is a famous, favorite psalm, attributed to the writing of King David, who himself fell into brambles and needed the Rescuer to lead him to the safety and rest this beautiful psalm describes. Here, Jehovah Raah, Our Shepherd, is described telling us, "This is who I AM".

Section Three

GOD THE SON, JESUS - I AM
The Good Shepherd

Through the prophets, God not only declares Himself to be a shepherd of His people, but He points to Jesus (in Ezekiel 34 and Isaiah 53) as the One coming from the line of David, the One who would make a way to gather the scattered wanderer back to the Good Shepherd and the safety and protection of His sheepfold.

In the New Testament Jesus Himself describes what it means for Him to be the Good Shepherd. He cares for the sheep and lays down His life for His sheep. He knows His sheep and His sheep know Him. Jesus protects and guides those who believe in Him. He is the Shepherd of all who put their trust in Him. John 6:63 tells us that it is the Good Shepherd who is able to give us life to the full.

"I have come that they may have life and have it to the full. I am the good shepherd. The good shepherd lays down his life for the sheep. The hired hand is not the shepherd and does not own the sheep. So, when he sees the wolf coming, he abandons the sheep and runs away. Then the wolf attacks the flock and scatters it. The man runs away because he is a hired hand and cares nothing for the sheep.

"I am the good shepherd; I know my sheep and my sheep know me - just as the Father knows me and I know the Father - and I lay down my life for the sheep." John 10:10-15 (NIV)

Here the Good Shepherd describes Himself as "good", pointing back to His righteousness. He is the Restorer. He is the One who cares enough about each individual, you and me, to die protecting and saving those who choose to follow Him and experience life to the full.

Adding this understanding of the Good Shepherd brings depth and even deeper meaning to Psalm 23.

He is always there to daily guide us as we ask Him to teach us and show us His ways.

"Show me your ways, O LORD,
teach me your paths;
guide me in your truth and teach me,
for you are God my Savior,
and my hope is in you all day long".
Psalm 25: 4&5 (NIV)

The fullness of life in Jesus comes as we pray and read His word. Yet both prayer and reading the Bible can feel lifeless and empty if we approach it only with our minds. Sometimes it's simply a thing to get checked off our daily list.

When we invite the Holy Spirit into our prayer or reading times, His Spirit can speak to our spirit and breathe life-giving guidance, understanding and hope into our very souls.

> **Prayer is the oxygen of the believer's soul.**

Prayer is simply talking to God from our inner most sanctuary. It is being honest with Him about the things that concern us, and it is releasing them into His loving hands for His guidance. It is a conversation with the LORD God Almighty and yet it is also a conversation with the One who calls us, "Friend". This is such an amazing privilege!

"I have called you friends, for everything I have learned from my Father I have made known to you." John 15:15 (NIV)

When we enter into conversation with God we don't need to flounder with words and wonder what to ask for. His word, the Bible, guides us and as we agree with His word we find power in prayer. We will find our prayers changing from desperate "Please! Please!" prayers for the solutions we desire to "Thank you! Thank you!" prayers for who He is, as we use His word to guide our praying.

> **The backbone of prayer is agreement with God's word.**

"Thank you, Father, that You are my good Shepherd. Thank you that You promise to go ahead of me and guide me. You offer me protection and provision of all I need. Help me today to rest in Your care. Show me the moments when I can linger in a "quiet meadow", pausing to ponder Your presence. Help me to trust You completely to lead me and also to follow me with Your goodness and mercy. I bring the cares on my heart to You now.... (name them) ... thanking You that You will guide me and keep me steady as we navigate the way together. Thank you that I can trust You to lead the way through the challenges.

Calm my heart with Your presence as I pray this in the strong name of Jesus, amen.

The Bible and prayer go hand in hand.
They are like two sticks of dynamite.

PAUSE & PONDER

Think about the time you spend in prayer and in reading God's word. It is an invitation to sit down and talk with the Lord about the things on our hearts. Psalm 23 says that even in the presence of our enemies, when things are hard and confusing, He sets a place for us to join Him. There we receive His peace and strength, His wisdom and guidance as we navigate the paths of our lives.

As we ponder the words of His promises, it gives us insight as to how to pray.

Section Four

GOD THE HOLY SPIRIT - OUR INTERCESSOR

When we find ourselves weak and not knowing where to turn or what to do next, we are reminded that the Holy Spirit is praying for us. He pleads on our behalf for God to intervene.

"In the same way, the Spirit helps us in our weakness. We do not know what we ought to pray for, but the Spirit himself intercedes for us through wordless groans. And he who searches our hearts knows the mind of the Spirit because the Spirit intercedes for God's people in accordance with the will of God". Romans 8:26,27

The Holy Spirit is the Revealer who gives us wisdom and knowledge as we navigate the paths of life. He leads us with the love of the kind Shepherd, even through valleys of loss. He calls us to His "table" even when we feel surrounded by hostility. He feeds us and cares for us. We can watch for His goodness and His mercy at our heels as we follow Him.

To think that the Spirit of the LORD intercedes for us is an amazing thought! The Scripture calls Him our Advocate, the One who steps in to intervene or mediate on our behalf. It is His power at work pushing back the darkness that shadows our way and often our minds. He pushes it back so we can see the Light and make the choice to follow His voice as He calls us out of darkness. His desire is for us to experience life more abundantly!

John 10:10 (NIV) tells us that Jesus said, *"The thief comes only to steal and kill and destroy: I have come that they may have life and have it more abundantly".* The sheep trust their Shepherd and He cares for them, leading them and guiding them, praying for them, saving them from, and in, trouble. What a comfort it is to know that He is praying for us, His treasured sheep, as we seek His paths.

John 6:63 (NIV) tells us that *"The Spirit gives life."*

What does it mean for us to be an "intercessor"? It is simply doing the same thing the Spirit does for us. It is praying for someone, asking the Spirit to guide our prayers as we intercede, asking the Holy Spirit to push back the darkness that is casting shadows on another's path. It is asking God to remove the blinders so they can see His love and light and be drawn to it. Each one of us always has free will to choose if we will follow Jesus. Yet, intercession can give that glimpse, that flicker of God's light calling an individual to follow the Good Shepherd, trusting His loving care to lead them where His love can take them.

PAUSE & PONDER

Ask the Spirit of God to nudge you when someone you care about needs prayer in a difficult or dark time. Ask the Lord to show you a scripture to share with them and to use as a guide in prayer.

Listen to this treasure from God's word. This is what I call a "camping verse". You can pitch your tent on this verse on a Monday morning when the week stretches in front of you with questions that puzzle you.

"The LORD will guide you always;
he will satisfy your needs in a sun-scorched land
and will strengthen your frame.
You will be like a well-watered garden,
like a spring whose waters never fail."
Isaiah 58:11 (NIV)

It's worth camping on.

"The LORD will guide you - ALWAYS.

He will satisfy your needs - in a sun-scorched land.
(Even when all around is barren and dry)

He will strengthen your frame.
(He offers all of Him to all of me)

You will be like a well-watered garden,
(Fragrant and flourishing)

like a spring whose waters never fail".
(Because He is the source)
Isaiah 58:11(NIV)

I have this verse underlined in my Bible. It is a great verse to write out or highlight somehow so it can continue to bring life to your soul as you go through your week. It helps raise the bar on our expectation of seeing God at work guiding us through our days, helping us bring His fragrance into our circles of influence. It helps open our eyes so we can see how the presence of the Good Shepherd can influence and guide our lives: our supper hour, our meetings, our phone calls, and the places and circumstances where we rub shoulders with others who also need the refreshing of the Spring that never fails.

He will guide us into His presence, to strengthen us where there is refreshing and the continual supply of His Spirit which is a spring that never fails.

As we choose to step out of the noise, making time to follow the Good Shepherd, we find Him there, ready to meet us, ready to lead us. As we allow Him to water our souls, cascading His lavish love and care over us, we are refreshed, and able to offer refreshing to others.

"Now thanks be to God who always leads us in triumph in Christ, and through us diffuses the fragrance of His knowledge in every place." 2 Corinthians 2:14 (NKJV)

Section Five

PRAYING THE 23RD PSALM (NKJV)

The Shepherd's Psalm for me

"The LORD is my shepherd; I shall not want."

Thank you, LORD, that You are the shepherd who leads the way for me. With You as my guide, I will have all that I need to walk this day.

"He makes me to lie down in green pastures; He leads me beside the still waters."

Thank you that You bring me to quiet waters and green meadows where I can rest and refresh. May I watch for them as You lead me. May I choose to pause and ponder Your presence there.

"He restores my soul; He leads me in the paths of righteousness for His name's sake."

Restore my soul. Refresh my mind and my emotions. Infuse my choices with what You desire for me. Lead me where my faith will flourish.

"Yes, even though I walk through the valley of the shadow of death, I will fear no evil; for You are with me; Your rod and staff they comfort me."

LORD, there is much loss around me, and shadows that darken the way. Thank you that I need not fear because You are with me every step. Your Shepherd's staff pulls me back from danger and fights off predators, gently nudging me in the right direction.

"You prepare a table before me in the presence of my enemies; You anoint my head with oil; my cup runs over."

Thank you that You prepare a feast for me as I turn to Your table, even as enemies of doubt and fear may lurk nearby. You anoint me with the oil of Your Spirit to heal me and reveal Your presence to me. You prepare me for the tasks You have for me. I am so thankful for You!

"Surely goodness and mercy shall follow me all the days of my life; and I will dwell in the house of the Lord forever."

PAUSE & PONDER

We can pause and thank God that He is our Good Shepherd. Think about where you need the most guidance right now. Thank Him that He has promised to guide you, always.

RELEASE to Him what it is that you need His guidance on. Roll the concern from your shoulders to His powerful hand. Speak it out to Him.

Psalm 23 and Isaiah 58:11 are good verses to use as prayer patterns.

Watch for Him to be at work as you rest in His "meadow". He has promised to guide you, to keep you as a well-watered garden. Trust Him as you wait and watch.

Because prayer is the oxygen of our souls and the word of God is the backbone of our prayers, here is another suggested prayer pattern I've found helpful in my quiet time with the LORD.

One Prayer Pattern to use in daily quiet time.

1. Start with thanking God for one of His names and all it reveals about His character. Ponder on that a bit. It helps lift the focus from what is going on around us, and onto His face, to who He is.

2. Clear the air between you and God and talk over any attitude, action or anxious worry that is stealing your peace. Ask Him to show you anything you need to be aware of.

3. Invite the Holy Spirit into your thoughts, your emotions and your choices, asking Him to guide you.

4. Enjoy some time reading the Bible or a devotional on His word. Ask the Lord what He wants to highlight to you. If something stands out to you ponder it and ask for His insight.

5. Look for any themes that might be emerging. Offer your day into God's hands, thanking Him for His presence with you and asking for greater awareness of Him as you move through the day. If a theme has emerged take it with you into your day.

6. Pray for any needs or concerns of the day and for the people you know you will encounter today. Thank the LORD that He goes ahead of you as your Guide.

Return, as you finish your quiet time, to the name of God you were focusing on, taking that awareness into your day. Using the names of God helps keep His face in focus to know Him better, to be refreshed in His presence and not simply looking to His hand to what we want Him to supply. He is the Good Shepherd. The Shepherd of our hearts.

He Guides Me

"The LORD will guide you always.
He will satisfy your needs in a sun-scorched land.
He will strengthen your frame.
You will be like a well-watered garden,
like a spring whose waters never fail." Isaiah 58:11 (NIV)

A WELL-WATERED GARDEN

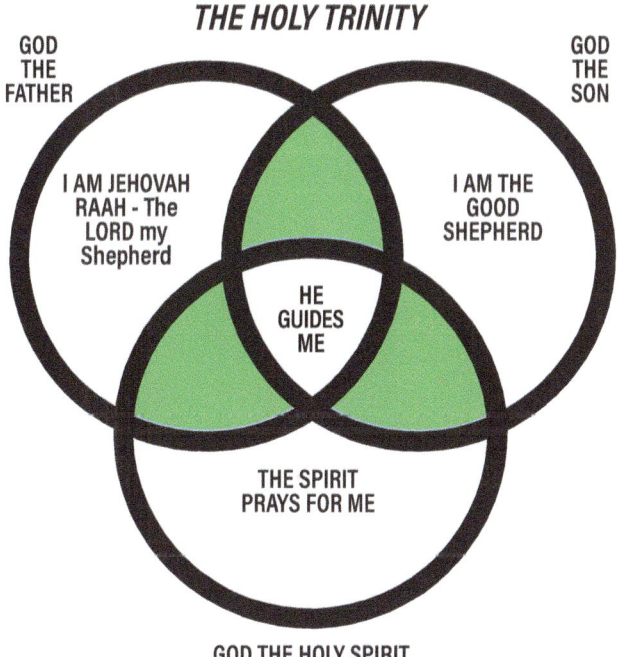

THE HOLY TRINITY

GOD THE FATHER

GOD THE SON

I AM JEHOVAH RAAH - The LORD my Shepherd

I AM THE GOOD SHEPHERD

HE GUIDES ME

THE SPIRIT PRAYS FOR ME

GOD THE HOLY SPIRIT

"He will guide you always...."

CHAPTER SIX

HE EQUIPS ME FOR BATTLE

GOD'S NAMES. GOD'S NATURE. GOD'S PROMISES.

CHAPTER SIX
Jehovah Nissi
He Equips Me for Battle

SECTION ONE
Belonging

The home hockey team was in the playoffs and banners were everywhere. They hung from the rafters of arenas, along fences in neighborhoods and on tee shirts and caps seen around town. Flags flew on poles and from truck antennas. The battle was on, and the moment was being highlighted and commemorated. Allegiance to the team was being declared boldly!

Banners honor all kinds of things: teams, events and victories. They mark celebrations of all kinds. They demonstrate an allegiance, a belonging that declares loyalty and support and often, victory!

GOD THE FATHER - Jehovah Nissi
The LORD my Banner
His Presence with me

Exodus 17 records a remarkable victory story. As the Israelites wandered through the desert searching for the Promised land, they encountered tribes who opposed their presence. At one point, the Israelites were being attacked by the Amalekites. Moses instructed Joshua (his apprentice) to take some men and head into the battle. It was a significant moment in their history.

Moses stood on a hill overlooking the battlefield and while Moses raised his arms over the field the Israelites gained ground. As he tired and his arms came down, the Amalekites gained ground. Moses' two companions, Aaron (his brother) and Hur saw what was happening and came alongside Moses. They set him on a rock to rest and with one on either side of him they held his arms up for the duration of the battle. The Israelites won and Moses acknowledged that it was God who had brought them victory.

Moses built an altar and named it, **"The Lord is My Banner"**. (Exodus 17:15) He was commemorating a battle and a victory, acknowledging the presence of the LORD in the midst of their struggle. His hands, extended over the battlefield, signified God's presence and banner over the Israelites. Moses was demonstrating their allegiance to the LORD. The LORD's banner, His protective covering over them, carried them to victory.

VICTORY

Later on, in Numbers 21, we see the Israelites under an attack of a different kind. In their own bitter complaining and impatience, they spoke out not only against Moses, but also against God.

This attitude against God brought on an unusual consequence of poisonous snakes. If bitten, death would be the result. As always, God has compassion on us in the stubborn attitudes of our hearts and He offers a rescue as He draws us back.

Here He instructed Moses to mount a bronze snake on a pole and, if bitten, anyone looking up to the pole would be healed of the poison. This was a way of acknowledging God in spite of the earlier speaking against Him.

This was also a foreshadowing of Jesus, a pointing to the One who would be lifted up on a cross to take the punishment for our selfish attitudes as we look to Him to rescue our hearts. He would also be lifted up from the grave, resurrected to life, offering new life and a new heart to all who believe.

This strange story depicts the attack from within. It reminds us how our own toxic attitudes can bring death to situations and relationships. Our own stubborn wills can turn too easily to speaking against not only others, but against God as well, blocking the hope and life He can bring.

The story of the battle with the Amalekites illustrates an outward attack from enemy forces, while this story in Numbers 21 reminds us that the inner battle is often subtler. Both stories remind us that acknowledging the LORD in the midst of our struggles is key.

Both stories illustrate the power of the name of the LORD as the Banner lifted over us in our battles. As Moses and his friends acknowledged God's presence with them in the physical act of holding up Moses hands, so it symbolizes keeping our eyes on the LORD instead of on our outer circumstances. Keeping a check on our hearts is wisdom if we want to stay on the path to victory. As we acknowledge the LORD's presence, in both our outer circumstances and our inner thoughts and attitudes, we can anticipate His rescue because of His reliable love for us.

"His banner over me is love." Song of Solomon 2:4 (NASB)

PAUSE & PONDER

It is interesting to think about where we tend to go when we feel "in the battle". It's easy to feel alone, seeking our own solutions and to simply react to what is going on around us.

Moses' example of acknowledging the LORD's presence in the midst of the circumstance brought his people victory. Considering how God's presence is with us, even in the heat of the moment, has the ability to change our reactions to more thoughtful responses as we lean into Him and not run to our own hasty solutions.

Often, we need friends to help keep us focused on God's presence with us, just as Moses had his friends who helped hold him up. God's banner over us is His love and presence with us, reminding us that we have a God whose reliable love has planned a rescue for us.

Who are the one or two people in your life to whom you could go for prayer and encouragement to help you keep your focus on God's presence even in the midst of challenges? Could you reach out to that person this week? Thank them that they are there to support you in prayer.

Psalm 20 further indicates God's hand in the affairs of people.

"May we shout for joy over your victory and lift up our banners in the name of our God. May the LORD grant all of your requests. Now this I know: The Lord gives victory to His anointed. He answers him from his heavenly sanctuary with the victorious power of his right hand.

"Some trust in chariots and some in horses, but we trust in the name of the LORD our God." Psalm 20:5-7 (NIV)

What power there is in trusting in the name of our LORD, the Almighty God, the Three in One Trinity! **The LORD our banner!**

We, as God's followers today can continue to say, "The Lord is my Banner," because it is under His Banner we take our stand, identified as belonging, as one loved and cared for by Our Heavenly Father. We are identified as His, part of His family, His team, we can stand in His authority and victory. We trust in His name, the name of the LORD our God. While others trust in the resources of their own gathering, He raises His banner over those who trust Him and who acknowledge His presence with them. He is trustworthy. His name is trustworthy!

Horses and chariots were the rich resources of the day. Today we have many other resources we can too easily tend to put our hope and confidence in. We might rely on our titles, positions, our money, social status, or our own strength and wisdom. No matter how limited or how abundant our earthly resources are, we can choose to trust in the all-powerful name of the LORD our God. Knowing that He is present with us changes our perspective and our expectations and draws us to look up instead of around when we feel the battle, the circumstances facing us, heating up.

Looking to the LORD our God instead of all that swirls around us, gives us confidence and hope as His presence brings His peace and His power. Looking at His resources instead of our own "chariots and horses" puts our confidence in His limitless grace and strength.

"Some trust in chariots and some in horses,
But we trust in the name of the LORD our God."
Psalm 20:7

SECTION TWO
God the Son, Jesus
I AM the Way, the Truth and the Life

Throughout the Old Testament, God the Father continually points to His Son, Jesus, and the fulfillment of the Old Testament prophecies of a Savior. God's heart to rescue is revealed over and over. Even here, in the name **Jehovah Nissi, The LORD our banner,** there is a foreshadowing of Jesus. As His name is lifted high, He becomes visible, and victory is possible in His name.

In the New Testament Jesus is quoted as saying, "***And I, when I am lifted up from the earth, will draw all people to myself." John 12:32 (NIV)***

Jesus Himself declared, "I AM the way, and the truth and the life". John 14:6 (NIV). As we lift the banner of His name over the things in our lives that need redemption, He shows us the way. He reveals truth to us, and He offers us abundant life, even in the midst of challenge. This is so much more than just "getting by" or "surviving".

In the face of attacks of all kinds we can consciously and intentionally raise the banner of the name of the LORD over us.

Whether we are dealing with internal conflict, confusion, doubt, or whether outside forces are prevailing against us in ways that rob us and seek to deplete and even destroy us, we can raise the banner of His name over us and our situations.

But what does it look like to raise His name and the banner of victory over our lives and our challenges on a Monday morning?

One thing I have found helpful has even changed my prayers. Though nothing may change around me, I have found this changes things within me. That makes all the difference. This is what I've learned:

As believers and followers of Jesus, we do not always recognize when we are in the midst of a battle. The news can worry us, situations can burden us, people can frustrate us and that is normal. We live in an imperfect world as imperfect people, in imperfect circumstances. Life happens. Even Jesus told us that in this world we will have trouble, but to take heart for He has overcome the world. (John 16:33) He equips us in the midst of it all.

Question marks swirl around us all the time, some are small, and some are far-reaching and huge. They can leave us feeling agitated and precarious.

Scripture tells us that not only will there be challenges and trouble in this world but also that we do have an enemy of our souls who comes to steal, kill and destroy. John 10:10 calls this enemy "The Thief". Few of us would debate the fact that there are times when we feel robbed of peace.

Other places in the Bible remind us to cast our cares on God, to be humble and to resist this thief. I Peter 5:8 gives us an amazing "heads up" in what to watch for as we seek to live in victory, day-to-day, even as we deal with the people and situations around us.

"Be alert and of sober mind. Your enemy the devil prowls around like a roaring lion seeking someone to devour."
1 Peter 5:8 (NIV)

This is a helpful word picture of a spiritual truth. Sometimes we are simply "eaten up / devoured" with things that drag us down. These are things like regret, guilt, anger, disappointment, grief, worry, fear, rejection, all leaving question marks that can tend to pull us under. Even our own choices and thoughts or habits can eat us up and pull us down.

When we find ourselves in the midst of a battle, where our adversary is using the things around us to rob us of our peace, we will be able to recognize it. We will find ourselves feeling that pull "under".

Under pressure.
Under stress.
Under the weather.
Under the circumstances.
Under a cloud.
Under fire.

You get the idea. We have all felt it.

That feeling of being "under" or "flat" due to something going on in us, to us or around us.

Things will often feel amplified and out of scope for what is actually going on. How we respond to it is the important thing. There is a thief who seeks to rob us of the victory Jesus secured for us at the cross. God offers us the opportunity to be fully alive, not dragged down by the things that try to creep into our hearts and pull us under.

Sometimes it is the outer battle of circumstances and sometimes it is the inner battle of hurt, pain, confusion and disappointment. Through Jesus, the Way, the Truth and the Life, God can cancel the pain we carry for the many ways we have trespassed against others through words, attitudes, actions and choices. He also offers healing for the way others have trespassed against us, causing us to carry hurts as well. As we bring our hurts to Him and invite Him into them, His Spirit brings clarity, forgiveness, strength and healing.

Colossians 2:13-15 is a victory cry that belongs to believers. God makes us alive with Christ. He forgives us, nailing all the trespasses, made by us and to us, to the cross. He has disarmed the thief!

"And having disarmed the powers and authorities, he made a public spectacle of them, triumphing over them by the cross".

Colossians 2:15 (NIV)

The thief has been disarmed. His roar of threat to devour us comes from a defeated foe, a toothless lion. Yet the noise is loud and the pull to "under" is real. This is when I find it wise to turn my gaze from around me to acknowledge God's presence with me and in me in whatever is eating away at me. This is where knowing His names helps us focus on who He is in us and for us.

We often find ourselves praying desperate "Please! Please!" prayers, anxious for God to intervene and remove what flattens us. We often believe that we know what the answer should be, and we beg God to comply with what we deem the best solution.

Yet the scripture gives us a different way to pray, which is counter intuitive. It tells us to be thankful. When we are "under" it feels impossible to reach to thanksgiving. There may seem to be little to give thanks for and, at times, that may be true. So, what should we do? We should turn our focus to the banner over us and we begin to thank God for who He is in the middle of the situation.

As we acknowledge His presence in the midst of where we are and turn our focus to thanking Him that He is present and that He lovingly has plans to bless us, we find ourselves emerging from "under". As we lift our eyes to Jesus, we find He offers us a way through the trial as He offers us His truth. As we turn our focus to thanking Him for all He is as He walks with us, it brings new life to our minds and hearts. As we acknowledge Him, He helps us acknowledge what is going on, not just around us, but in us as well.

Our desperate "Please! Please!" prayers change to expectant "Thank you! Thank you!" prayers and we find a shift happens within us, even if nothing changes around us.

PAUSE & PONDER

Think about one situation that causes you concern these days. It can be anything from a strained relationship to world news, interest rates, health concerns or anything that occupies your mind and heart with a little or a lot of angst.

Reframe that concern putting God in the middle of the picture. Acknowledge His presence with you and in you and in the situation.

Turn your thoughts to prayer and instead of asking Him for your best solution to the situation, begin to thank Him for His presence with you in this. Thank Him for His plans to bless you, for His wisdom to guide you and for His peace to flood your heart and mind as you wait on Him in the situation.

Trusting Him, having faith in His presence and power with us, is the victory. Peace is the amazing result as we walk through battles of many kinds.

SECTION THREE

God the Holy Spirit

His Power

As the LORD leads us through our day-to-day journey, we will encounter joys and challenges mingled together. His Spirit is there to transform us and strengthen us in our weaknesses. We do not walk alone. Our faith in the LORD sets the banner of victory over us. His Spirit prays through us as we pray. (Ephesians 6:18 NIV)

"For everyone born of God overcomes the world. This is the victory that has overcome the world, even our faith." 1 John 5:4 (NIV)

Walking in step with the Spirit of the Living God is to keep our eyes on that banner over us, to be reminded of His faithfulness to us and His joy in our faithfulness to Him.

It is not so much "who" we are as "whose" we are. The focus is on Him. Our faith in Him overcomes the things that threaten to distract, discourage, depress and even at times, destroy us.

"Since we live by the Spirit, let us keep in step with the Spirit."
Galatians 5:25 (NIV)

Keeping in step with the Spirit means looking to Him step by step to guide us and empower us in all we are doing. When we keep in step with someone walking beside us, we are able to converse and share the journey and the conversation. So, it is with God the Holy Spirit. Jesus called Him our "Comforter", our "Advocate", our "Helper", the One who prays for us, the One who walks with us. HIs Spirit whispers to our spirit and nudges us in the ways that are best for us and the ways that will bring blessing and peace. He leads us in wisdom that comes from above that is not "self-focused" but is peace-loving. James 3:14-18. As our constant companion, we can be assured of His help and comfort and support as He transforms us to be fully alive even as we walk through challenges.

It is easy to get caught up in the day and the moment and in the atmosphere around us. When we recognize that the atmosphere is negative, fear-filled, anxious and less than peaceful, we can invite the Holy Spirit of God to make His presence known through us. He will first quiet our own hearts as we invite Him. He will give us peace to share, words that bring healing rather than hurt, the ability to speak life when it is needed and to be silent when that is best.

This third person of the Trinity is our gift from the Father, through the Son and is with us and in us constantly. We need only ask for a deeper awareness of His presence, His peace and His power.

> *Jesus said,* **"And I will ask the Father, and he will give you another Advocate, who will never leave you." John 14:16 (NLT2)**

The events, interactions and the news of the day can consume us. The thief who comes to rob us will use these things to try to devour us. Yet God in His fullness has provided everything we need as we trust in His name and all He is for us. Every morning His love and compassion are fresh and new, offering all we need from all that He is!

> **"Because of the LORD's great love we are not consumed, for his compassions never fail. They are new every morning; great is your faithfulness." Lamentations 3:22,23 (NIV)**

Because of the LORD's great love, we are not consumed. What an amazing statement that is! We are not consumed, not eaten up, not devoured! We have His Banner of love and victory flying over us.

As we keep in step with God's Spirit, keeping Him in focus, we will be able to navigate the challenges that come our way. Where we focus, we follow.

Three-legged Stability

As with the old-fashioned three-legged milk stool, or the three -legged tripod stand, three legs provide a stable and firm place to rest even on uneven ground.

With the Trinity we have all three. They cannot be separated. They give us stability and balance, a firm place to stand. We need all three.

- God - The Promise Keeper, Our Rescuer, offers us His presence.
- Jesus -The Savior, Our Redeemer, offers us HIs peace as He buys back our broken pieces.
- Holy Spirit- The Spirit of Truth, The Revealer, sets us on the right course, leading the way to victory as we keep in step with Him.

Some believe in God but not Jesus. Others believe in Jesus but not in the active leading of the Holy Spirit. The Banner over us encompasses all three. The picture can only begin to be grasped in its fullness when we look at all three. This is where we find a firm place to stand when on the uneven ground of the battles, both within and without.

Ephesians 3:16-19 addresses all three, the Father, the Son, Christ Jesus, and the Holy Spirit.

"I pray that out of THE FATHER'S glorious riches he may strengthen you with power through his SPIRIT in your inner being, so that CHRIST may dwell in your hearts through faith.

And I pray that you, being rooted and established in love, may have power, together with all the Lord's holy people, to grasp how wide and long and high and deep is the love of Christ, and to know this love that surpasses knowledge—that you may be filled to the measure of all the fullness of God."

Ephesians 3:16-19 (NIV)

SECTION FOUR

A snapshot from our photo album

We had taken on a hangar and a dozen aircraft along with the routes and charters in another northern community. This time there was a road in and out. It was a big bite. We decided it would be best to live in the top of the hangar until we could purchase a house. So, we moved. With three children and a dog we established ourselves on the airport as "the hangar family". After the moving truck left and I got a close look at the top floor of the hangar, I was deflated. One of the children had a hard time adjusting to this unusual home. It was busy and noisy. I found myself in tears a lot of the time that first month. I knew it was a good decision and had readily agreed to the unusual arrangement. It made sense. Yet my heart could not find the enthusiasm it needed to make this adjustment. All my positive thinking and trying hard did not change the flattened state I was in.

About a month in I knew I could not carry on this way. It was eating me up. I was being devoured by my circumstances. So, I did what I always do when I don't know what to do, and that is to pray. I invited God into this inner chaos. His Spirit reminded me of the verse in Lamentations I knew well, "***Because of the LORD's great love we are not consumed, for His compassions never fail. They are new every morning; great is your faithfulness.***" I knew thanksgiving was the pathway out of this despair.

Why I waited to acknowledge God's presence and help in the situation, I do not know. It seems that we often think we can pull ourselves out of the various pits we find ourselves in. But I knew the route out was thanksgiving.

So, I began to turn my heart and my thoughts to thanking God. It was intentional, a choice I made. At first it was simply thankfulness for the sunshine, but thankfulness grows in our hearts as we practice it. I was thankful that we were all together on this new adventure. Though nothing changed immediately, it did change. My focus turned to not only thanking God for things like the sunshine or the blessings I could uncover each day, but to thanking Him for who He was in me and for me and with me as I chose to simply trust His love and care for us each day. God changed my heart as I turned my focus to Him. As we look back, those years in our hangar home hold some of our fondest memories as a family.

When we change our "please, please" prayers, begging our own solutions, to "thank you, thank you" prayers for who God is in our situations and in us, it can truly feel like a sacrifice when our emotions are far from praise. Yet that choice to turn to prayers of thanksgiving actually brings us into His presence in a profound way. They actually help prepare the way for God to show us His ways of rescue and salvation.

"He who offers a sacrifice of praise and thanksgiving honors Me; And to him who orders his way rightly [who follows the way I lead him], I shall show the salvation of God."
Psalm 50:23 (AMP)

"You will keep him in perfect peace, whose mind is stayed on You, because he trusts in You." Isaiah 26:3 (NKJV)

We thank Him that He has made Himself available to us. He offers all of Him to all of me!

- We thank Him that He is trustworthy, that He is kind.

- We thank Him that we can trust His goodness even when we cannot see it in the moment.

- We thank Him that He is with us in this, and that we can rely on His love.

- We thank Him that He will guide us and give us wisdom as we walk.

- We thank Him that He is sovereign over all things and that He will work things out for His glory and our good as we trust Him.

- We thank Him that He is all powerful, full of mercy and goodness.

- We thank Him that He reigns in justice and love, that He rescues, restores and reveals His presence.

- We thank Him for His peace and rest even in the midst of uncertainty and turmoil.

Thanksgiving for who our God is, in all His majesty, can be a battleground, especially if we find ourselves under attack from within or without, deflated for whatever reason. We can choose to turn our focus from the circumstance around us to thankfulness for the God within us and see what a difference His presence makes as we focus on Him right where we walk.

We can look at God through the telescope, feeling Him distant and small, while we magnify the details of our challenges in the microscope.

OR

We can look at God through the microscope and magnify the details of all He is, while we look at our problems through the telescope, keeping them in the distance.

> *"Oh, magnify the LORD with me,*
> *And let us exalt His name together."*
> *Psalm 34:3 (NKJV)*

Sometimes, when we desperately feel we need God's intervention, we do our very best thinking for God and then earnestly plead with Him for that specific solution. When the answer for which we had prayed does not come, our faith can be shaken, and we can easily distance our God who sees more than we do and whose love is constant and reliable.

Yet when we choose to trust Him and lean into all that His names reveal about His nature, we find a strength, an assurance, a peace that holds us, unshaken, even as things around us may shake.

Putting our faith in God the Father and in His Son, Jesus, gives us access to His Spirit who is our Advocate, our strength and our assurance through the battles of life.

This is a strength that is beyond our own. This is divine help from the living and Almighty God, available as we turn to Him and trust Him. Often it is tempting to run from God when we do not understand what is happening. Yet running to Him in childlike faith leads us to victory.

"This is the victory that has overcome the world, even our faith. "

1 John 5:4 (NIV).

PAUSE & PONDER

How do I tend to think of God when I am troubled or stressed? Is He distant, or near, giving a glimpse of the divine mystery right where I walk?

When I feel "in the battle", in challenging outward circumstances, or inner struggles feeling "under", I can draw on God's strength and power, and on His wisdom through pondering His promises and inviting Him into my circumstances, thoughts and decisions. What a privilege this is!

If I am particularly overwhelmed, do I need to talk to a trusted friend, pastor or counsellor to pray with me and walk with me on my journey to wholeness?

LORD GOD,

Thank you that Your name is the banner that flies over me. I can lift my eyes and see Your name and all that You are. LORD, Your word says You know that we are made of dust, and You have compassion on us in our wanderings.

Thank you that You seek to redeem and restore me and reveal Yourself to me. Thank you that You will reveal the way I should go. May I keep in step with Your Spirit today. When my concerns seek to overwhelm me LORD, remind me of who You are. As I wait for You to work in my circumstances, I thank you that You will steady me. Give me Your thoughts and infuse my choices with Your desires. May I lean hard into all You are. Thank you for all You offer me as I walk through my day.

Please help me to keep You under the microscope, marveling at Your care and attention. May Your peace be magnified in my heart. May I lift my eyes first to You to see Your loving face before I let the problems and cares of the day cast their shadows.

Thank you that You desire to establish Your kingdom in my life. May Your kingdom be established in me and through me today, and in the lives of those whose names I bring before you now.

(Name those for whom you are carrying a burden and release them to the care of Jesus.)

Thank you for all that Your banner means as it flies over me today. I thank you and I pray in the strong name of Jesus. Amen.

Note to Reader:

If you are struggling under a weight that feels impossible to get out from under, please find someone trustworthy to talk and pray with. We are not meant to journey alone. Ask God to remind you of a friend, pastor or counsellor you can reach out to.

The backbone of prayer is agreement with God's word. This is a spiritual truth to remember and to put into practice.

Scripture reminds us that our struggle is against spiritual forces. Though the thief, the enemy of our souls, may use people against us, the battle is in the heavenly realms and the battle is the LORD'S.

"For our struggle is not against flesh and blood, but against the rulers, against the authorities, against the powers of this dark world and against the spiritual forces of evil in the heavenly realms."

Ephesians 6:12 (NIV)

Pray the Scripture. God's word has power.

LORD, thank you that though some may trust in the horses and chariots of our day, trusting in finances, political parties, titles, possessions and positions, You have instructed me to trust in Your name alone.

Thank you that because of Your great love, I do not have to be consumed. May I recall your faithfulness, the mercies you give me daily and the strength and power in Your name.

Thank you that You are the Banner over me today. May I focus there, relying on Your love and on who You are as I release my cares to You. Amen.

"This is the victory that has overcome the world, even our faith." 1 John 5:4 (NIV)

PAUSE & PONDER

When we look with spiritual eyes at the things going on in and around us, we can be encouraged that God has equipped us for the battle. He gives divine power to pull down strongholds (2 Corinthians 10:3-5). He helps us with the passions that tend to pull us under. (James 4) and He reminds us that "greater is He who is in us than He who is in the world." (1John 4:4) These are great scriptures to pitch our tent on, equipping us to stand firm in who our Jehovah Nissi is for us, the Banner over us.

"The name of the LORD is a fortified tower,
The righteous run to it and are safe."
Proverbs 18:10 (NIV)

"Some trust in chariots and some in horses,
but we trust in the name of the LORD our God"
Psalm 20:7 (NIV)

"Above all, taking the shield of
faith with which you will be able to quench all the
fiery darts of the wicked one."
Ephesians 6:16 (NIV)

Thank you, Lord, for Your protective armor over me.

Ephesians 6:10-18 says, *"Put on the full armor of God, so that when the day of evil comes, you may be able to stand your ground, and after you have done everything to stand....*

- *"Stand firm then with the Belt of Truth buckled around your waist...* Lord, please give me understanding of what is true and right in every situation I walk into today.

- *"With the Breastplate of Righteousness in place...* Lord, I thank You that I am loved by you and that you have washed my resistance to You away and covered my doubt.

- *"And with your feet fitted with the readiness that comes from the Gospel of Peace....* Lord, remind me today to be open to what you want me to do; use my hands and feet and show me people you would have me show special kindness to today.

- *"In addition to all this, take up the Shield of Faith, with which you can extinguish all the flaming arrows of the evil one.....* Lord, I thank you that by faith in Your power I can be protected from temptation and wrong desires today. Guide me and protect me. Keep me from temptation and increase my faith in You.

- *"Take up the Helmet of Salvation...* Lord, I celebrate the fact that I am your child and Your banner of victory and love is over me.

- *"and the Sword of the Spirit, which is the Word of God....* Lord, give me the desire to read your Word. Help me not to just read it but to obey it too.

- *"And pray in the Spirit on all occasions with all kinds of prayers and requests....* Lord, guide my day and gently remind me to bring my problems to You as they arise, remembering to turn my "Please! Please!" to Thank you for all You are in me and in my circumstances.

- *"**With this in mind, be alert and always keep on praying for all the saints....**"* Lord, keep me alert and focused on You today, praying for others too, for You are our hope! Amen.

He Equips Me for Battle

"The name of the LORD is a fortified tower the righteous run to it and are safe." Proverbs 18:10 (NIV)

EQUIPPED FOR THE BATTLES OF LIFE

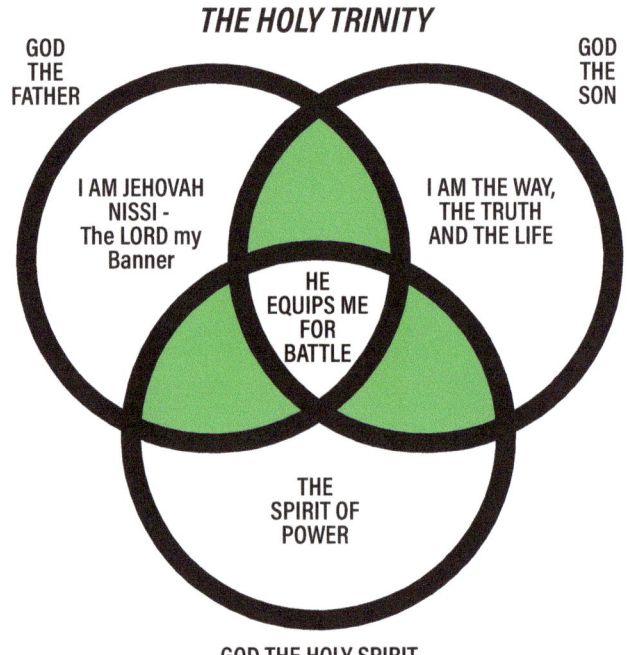

THE HOLY TRINITY

GOD THE FATHER

GOD THE SON

I AM JEHOVAH NISSI - The LORD my Banner

I AM THE WAY, THE TRUTH AND THE LIFE

HE EQUIPS ME FOR BATTLE

THE SPIRIT OF POWER

GOD THE HOLY SPIRIT

"Some trust in chariots and some in horses, but we trust in the name of the LORD our God." Psalm 20:7

CHAPTER SEVEN

HE SUSTAINS ME

GOD'S NAMES. GOD'S NATURE. GOD'S PROMISES.

SECTION ONE
God the Father - Jehovah Jireh
My Provider
A snapshot from our album

We had never been to the jungles of South America. We felt it was worth taking the kids out of school for this educational trip. We were to visit a project that would involve a day trip in the Andes Mountains. We were excited. The local driver assigned to us that day seemed familiar with the area. We headed out early in the morning. The scenery was breath-taking. We were amazed at the narrow road with just enough room for two vehicles to pass, the hairpin turns and places where the drop-off of hundreds of feet made the trees below look like tiny LEGOLAND trees. I prayed again for safety.

Suddenly, around one tight turn we met a bus. It took the whole road, and we were forced off. Thankfully, at that point in the road there was a rolling ditch only a few feet deep rather than a sharp drop off. Our vehicle rolled completely over and came to rest on its side in the ditch of dense brush. I remember seeing a parrot in a bus window as it sped away. The driver did not even slow down to see if we were alright.

We got out, shook the glass off the children and ourselves, checked everyone over and were so thankful to all be intact. The children and I climbed up out of the ditch while John was survey-ing the area for some logs he could use to get the vehicle turned over and back up the embankment.

I noticed a man coming down the side of the mountain across from the ditch while a woman peered out from among the trees higher up. He came with his machete and began to cut the dense brush around the vehicle.

As I stood watching I did the only thing I know to do, when I don't know what to do, and that is to pray. In the few hours we had been on that road the bus had been the only other traffic.

As the men worked and I prayed suddenly around that hair pin corner came a pick-up truck with four big strapping boys from Toronto! Do angels wear Bermuda shorts? I was sure they did! With their help John was able to get the vehicle back on the road and headed back in the direction we had come. Amazingly the vehicle worked.

It was a long drive back up the mountain road, darkness was coming, and rain was pelting through the hole where the windshield had been. John was driving now which felt better. We saw no other traffic. As darkness fell and we reached the edge of the city a tire went flat. We were on a street that had a tire shop, still open, right across from where we happened to be. Even a half hour earlier that flat tire would have made for an incredibly challenging situation on that mountain road in the dark.

We were thankful to get back to our hotel that night. We realized the miraculous day we had experienced. We were thankful to God! Thankful that we were not injured, thankful for my cool, calm husband who knew what to do next. We were thankful for the angels from Toronto, thankful that the vehicle started, thankful the tire had not gone flat earlier. We were so very thankful that God's hand of provision had been with us in so many ways that day.

God provides for us in so many different ways. Often, we don't even recognize them. One name of God the Father is, **Jehovah Jireh**, meaning "my provider". It comes out of a rather strange and interesting story in the Old Testament in Genesis chapter 22. The backstory is equally as interesting.

Back in Genesis 12 we have the account of God speaking to Abraham. He was called Abram at that time and he and his wife Sarai, along with his father and his nephew Lot were living in Harran where they had settled. (Modern day Turkey). In Abram's account of God speaking to him we don't have the same kind of details that were recorded when God later spoke to Moses by the burning bush. Nevertheless, his call was no less dramatic in that God spoke and called Abram to leave his father and go to a land God would show him. Abram was not a young man, and this would have been a huge leap of faith to go, not knowing where, but because God had said, "Go".

Yet God did not just give Abram instruction without also giving him His promise to go with it.

The LORD had said to Abram,
"Go from your country, your people and your father's
household to the land I will show you.
"I will make you into a great nation, and I will bless you;
I will make your name great, and you will be a blessing..."

Genesis 12:1-3 (NIV)

God's word to Abram was strong and firm.
"I will show you the land."
"I will make you into a great nation."
"I will bless you."
"I will make your name great."
"I will bless those who bless you."
"I will bless all people through you."

God's word was enough for Abram. Nothing but faith and obedience were required on his part. The rest was God's part. God said, "I will" over and over. Abram took his family and all his possessions and the people who worked with him and embarked on his journey. We can only imagine the difficult journey, by foot, across diverse terrain. What courage it must have taken to begin that step of faith! The scripture tells us that along the way God appeared to Abram and said, "This land will be your offspring's land." Abram stopped and built an alter to the LORD. At another place he stopped again and built an alter to the LORD and called upon His name. All along his journey he kept focused on the God who was leading him.

There was a lot of drama and excitement along the way. Eventually Abram settled in the region south of Jerusalem. Lot had gone in another direction. Abram settled in, still believing God's promise to him that this land would one day belong to his offspring in spite of the fact that his wife was barren. God appeared to him again and changed his name from "Abram" meaning "Father", to "Abraham" meaning "Father of Nations".

Yet no heir was in sight and both Abraham and his wife were now very old.

Eventually Sarai, whose name God changed to Sarah, had a miracle baby. The story is riveting in its detail. Isaac was born. He was the promised heir, the promise to Abraham that had finally come to pass. Through Isaac God would bless all people on earth. This was a foreshadowing of the coming Christ. Through the line of Abraham there was One coming to offer blessing and healing to all people on earth.

Isaac grew. The story continues to the strange account where one day God instructed Abraham to take Isaac up the mountain and offer him as a sacrifice him. What a bizarre turn of events this was. This offspring had been promised by God and waited for so long, the one through whom blessing was promised to come. Yet Abraham was a man full of faith in God. When his son asked him where the lamb was for the offering that they were going up to make, Abraham replied that, "God Himself will provide the lamb".

Abraham's faith in God and His promise was unshakable. He had been sustained by God many times and had seen God intervene too many times to doubt that He would again. In Hebrews 11:9 it tells us that Abraham reasoned that if Isaac were to die, God could bring him back to life. He trusted unwaveringly in this God he had grown to know so well.

In James 2:23 (NIV) it tells us, "Abraham believed God, and it was credited to him as righteousness, and he was called God's friend".

God did provide a lamb for the sacrifice at just the right moment. It was there, in that moment with his son, Isaac when a lamb bleated from behind a bush, that Abraham referred to God as Jehovah Jireh, my Provider. God indeed provided as Abraham trusted Him.

God, our Provider, was pointing to the future, to Jesus, God's son, who would come to be sacrificed as the perfect lamb, providing redemption and blessing for all humankind.

Abraham is such an amazing example of faith. All along his journey full of question marks of where he was going, he trusted God and built alters along the way, keeping his focus on God's faithfulness.

PAUSE & PONDER

When life is filled with questions and the way ahead seems uncertain, we do well to keep our focus on God's faithfulness. God's provision can be counted on. Gathering with others and hearing their stories of God's faithfulness can encourage us along the way.

As Abraham and his family traversed the land, longing for a home to settle in, God provided courage, faith and guidance as Abraham trusted Him to lead them.

When circumstances are not what we had hoped for, and the way is obscured, God can be trusted to provide all the perseverance, strength and courage we need as we trust Him to guide us along the way.

Section Two

God the Son

"I AM the Bread of Life"

God the Son, Jesus, declared Himself to be "The Bread of Life". Jesus Himself promises to sustain us, nourish us and give us what we need daily.

During the time of Moses when the Israelites were wandering in the desert looking for the promised land, they were hungry. There was little to sustain them. God provided manna, bread on the ground every morning. They were instructed to take only a day's supply, because the rest would spoil. Exodus 16 tells the story.

With the same emphasis on the dailyness of God's supply, we see this pattern in the Lord's Prayer. ***"Give us this day our daily bread"***. Matt. 6.

God's provision is for today. Jesus said in John 6:35 that whoever comes to Him will never hunger again. He satisfies that spiritual hunger within us, that hunger for something more that is undefinable, and is met when we invite Jesus into our lives. He satisfies that hunger deep within as we, "Taste and see that the LORD is good". Psalm 34:8 (NIV)

In John 6 we have the familiar story of the feeding of the 5,000. The crowds followed Jesus listening intently to His teaching. Jesus told them, **"The bread of God is the bread that comes down from heaven and gives life to the world"**. Jesus was referring to Himself, yet the people thought he meant literal bread. **"Sir, always give us this bread",** they responded.

"Jesus declared, "I am the Bread of life. Whoever comes to me will never go hungry, and whoever believes in me will never be thirsty." " John 6:35 (NIV)

The vast part of the crowd was following Jesus hoping to get this "bread" in order to get their own physical hunger satisfied. They missed the point of what Jesus was telling them, that He was the one who would satisfy the deep inner needs of their souls. When more bread was not forthcoming, they lost interest.

Many of us look to Jesus for an instant miracle, an urgent physical need to be met. And His gracious love often provides for that need in the moment. He wants us to truly see Him and believe in Him. Yet when the urgency is past, or if He didn't meet the need in the way we had hoped or expected, we can lose interest too and miss the point of His presence, turning away in disappointment.

Or we can choose to shift our gaze from His hand and what we desired, to His face, knowing His love is reliable and His presence can fill us and satisfy us as we camp on the power and beauty of His promises. As we spend time listening to what He has to say to our hearts we experience His amazing presence. He is full of grace and truth. He comforts and strengthens us, gives wisdom in the darkness of circumstances as He brings light to our souls. His plan is always for our good and His glory.

His presence fills us and satisfies us.

Jesus reminded the crowd, ***"Do not labor for the food which perishes, but for the food which endures to everlasting life, which the Son of Man will give to you because God the Father has set His seal on Him." John 6:27 (NKJV)***

God sent Jesus to give us life abundantly! Life to the full!

"The thief comes only to steal and kill and destroy; I have come that they may have life, and have it to the full." John 10:10 (NIV)

Jesus not only offers eternal life when this earthly life is over, but on this earth, He gives us the provision of His character within us to navigate our days. Just as our bodies need daily bread to sustain us, we need the daily refreshing of God's word and time spent with Him. He truly is the Bread of Life, our Sustainer, our Nourisher, our Provider, who offers us His presence daily. Come to the table.

God is ever only one prayer away!

I love the miracle story in John 6 of the little boy offering his lunch to Jesus. In my mind's eye I can see the day growing long as the crowds followed Jesus. Jesus asked some of His disciples where they could get food to feed them. There was no town nearby and the cost to buy food for that crowd would have been too expensive anyway.

One of the disciples, Andrew, stepped forward and said there was a little boy there with five barley loaves and two small fish, but what good was that among so many?

I can just imagine the little boy overhearing the disciples talking about feeding the crowd. Clutching the small lunch, I can see him tugging on Andrew's coat. "You can have my lunch".

Imagine the life-changing experience this little guy would have had as he watched Jesus take his lunch from Andrew, pray over it and give it to the disciples to pass out. Incredibly everyone got their fill and there were twelve basketfuls left over!

What we have can feel inadequate for the need that is in front of us. Yet simple childlike faith can offer it to Jesus and watch the outcome. Instead of frustration at the inadequacy, faith can move mountains as we place our "small lunch bag" in the hands of Jesus and ask Him to bless it and multiply it. Trusting Him, putting our faith into action, believing that He is with us and in us makes all the difference.

Often, we look into our own "lunch bags" and see barely enough to sustain us for the day. Yet Jesus said, "The bread of God comes down from Heaven and gives life to the world". John 6:33

When we offer what we have to Jesus, as inadequate as it may feel, He in turn multiplies it and even feeds others through us. He gives us stories to tell of His provision and His presence. The bread of life that He offers us fills us on the inside in ways we never imagined.

PAUSE & PONDER

Is there a place of hunger within you today? Is there a place where scarcity threatens your view of God? Invite Jesus, the Bread of Life to come in and satisfy your longings with all He is. Offer what you do have to Him and see what He will do with it. We need not be parched and hungry as we navigate the challenges of life. He has all we need to sustain us. We need only ask.

Section Three

God the Holy Spirit

He produces fruit in my life

Our own daily hunger is a good reminder that yesterday's manna, yesterday's experience of Jesus in our lives, yesterday's nourishment will not quench todays need. We must go to the Father, through Jesus, relying on His Spirit to feed us, craving what only He can provide.

"Like newborn babies, crave pure spiritual milk, so that by it you may grow up in your salvation, now that you have tasted that the Lord is good." 1 Peter 2:2&3 (NIV)

As our Provider, God the Holy Spirit produces "fruit in our lives". The nourishment of knowing Jesus as our Savior, the Bread of Life, introduces His Spirit who produces the fruit that identifies us as God's children.

Matthew 7:17-20 (NIV) tells us to watch for the fruit. *"Every good tree bears good fruit. By their fruit you will recognize them".* It is a filter worth paying attention to both in our own lives and in the lives of those we connect with. Watch for the fruit.

"But the fruit of the Spirit is love, joy, peace, patience, kindness, goodness, faithfulness, gentleness and self-control; against such things there is no law." Galatians 5:22,23 NIV

God the Holy Spirit produces in us what we need to be sustained daily, as we ask: "Give us this day our daily bread". It is supernatural!

PROVIDER. SUSTAINER. NOURISHER.

> ### *PAUSE & PONDER*
>
> *Read again that list of spiritual fruits in the verse above. Choose one fruit of the Spirit that you feel lacking in and ask God today to work in you through His Holy Spirit to increase it.*
>
> *When you encounter a toxic, harsh, or negative spirit, in yourself or in others, ask the Holy Spirit to help you cooperate with Him and respond in the opposite spirit. It is His work. You just make the choice and send the invitation!*

Work was not what we had anticipated that year. I don't recall being overly anxious about it, but I do recall inviting Jesus into my grocery shopping. Every week before I went to the grocery store, I would ask Him to give me wisdom in my shopping. Every bag of groceries I brought into the kitchen I said a silent "thank you" for. Friends shared garden produce. The ladies that came for Bible study brought cake and cookies. We were aware of God's provision. That winter I won a draw for a meat hamper at the grocery store. We didn't live in "lack". We had a deep sense of God's abundance.

A friend needed to hire some babysitting, and I was able to provide it. This was an unexpected blessing, including that of playmates for our children and a noon hour visit with my friend as she took her lunch break with us. Our visits often turned to things of God, and we were both blessed.

Oh, it was busy and the after-school rush of getting four children ready to go pick up two more from school could be a challenge, especially with snowsuits and boots!

Looking back, the Tuesday morning Bible study group was a definite provision of God too. I could not attend the weekly ladies' group at the church due to the babysitting, so four grannies came to my house. They didn't mind the noise and occasional chaos of the children playing in the next room. They each knew Jesus well and I learned so much that winter from their comments, their stories and the way they prayed. He provides what we need even when we are unaware of His hand directing our lives.

Through a challenging year we experienced God's goodness and provision. And our hearts were filled with gratitude.

"See how the flowers of the field grow. They do not labor or spin...Therefore do not worry... For your heavenly Father knows that you need all these things..." Matthew 6:28-34 (NIV)

I find that when I take the time to intentionally invite the life-flowing power of the Spirit into each circumstance and decision, the fruit begins to show!

We make a choice each day, as followers of Jesus, to either operate in our own strength or to co-operate with the power of the Holy Spirit, asking Him to bring an abundant harvest of fruit into our lives. The sweetness of this fruit will reveal Jesus to those around us.

We can be sure that God will always supply our need to be strengthened and sustained in the moment and in the day where we walk. We need only to trust him to walk with us. His provision may not always look like we anticipate but He will meet us in our need.

God will always meet the deep needs of our hearts as we navigate the challenges of life and take time to look into His face, and not just at His hand. He will supply all we need to be strengthened in our inner being.

"And my God will meet all your needs according to the riches of his glory in Christ Jesus." Philippians 4:19 (NIV)

PAUSE & PONDER

Spend a few minutes thinking about the need that is upper-most on your heart and mind these days. Thank God that He has promised to be Jehovah Jireh to you, your Provider, in this very need. Thank Him that you can trust His goodness in this. Thank Him that He has all you need for this particular situation. Thank Him that you can rely on Him.

Ask Him to help you trust Him and not simply lean on your own understanding. Thank Him that He will do what is best for your good and His glory. Thank Him for patience as you wait to see how He will provide for you and in you!

"Those who hope in the LORD will renew their strength. They will soar on wings like eagles; they will run and not grow weary, they will walk and not be faint." Isaiah 40:31 (NIV)

Heavenly Father,

Thank you for the gift of Your Holy Spirit to empower me with the fruit I so desperately need in my life.

Thank you that You know the needs I have daily, and You have said I do not need to worry.

Thank you that You also know my inner needs. Your word reminds me that Your strength is made perfect in my weakness. (2 Corinthians 12:9). May I begin to see my weaknesses not as areas to make me feel defeated, or to hide from myself or others. Help me to see them as the very entry point of Your grace and Your power to strengthen me with Your might in my weak places.

Lord, please help me today to acknowledge my weakness, to invite You into that place and experience the amazing power of Your Spirit providing for me.

Today I bring my outer needs to You, thanking you for Your provision. I also bring my inner needs to You, thanking you for strengthening me in my inner being. Grow in me the fruit of Your Spirit, I pray, with thanksgiving and in the strong name of Jesus, Amen.

All too easily we can see the weaknesses in one another often before we see our own. As I invite the Holy Spirit into my weak areas, may I also pray for those whose weaknesses I see. May I be diligent in praying for those I love. May I intercede in prayer for them. May I ask the Holy Spirit to push back the darkness that clouds not only my own vision, but the vision of those for whom I care deeply.

May we grow in trusting God to infuse our weak areas with the power of the Holy Spirit, to enlarge our faith and to keep us running to Him for His provision in our needs. It can feel easy to be tempted to run from God as we face our outward needs that can be overwhelming and, as we face frustrations in ourselves and in others. Yet He is the safe and empowering place to go. He offers His hand to steady us even when things around us are shaking. **Our hearts rejoice in His presence and provision.**

"I pray that out of His glorious riches He may strengthen you with power through His Spirit in your inner being, so that Christ may dwell in your hearts through faith.

And I pray that you, being rooted and established in love, may have power, together with all the Lord's holy people, to grasp how wide and long and high and deep is the love of Christ, and to know this love that surpasses knowledge— that you may be filled to the measure of all the fullness of God.

Now to Him who is able to do immeasurably more than all we ask or imagine, according to His power that Is at work within us, to Him be glory in the church and in Christ Jesus throughout all generations, for ever and ever! Amen."
Ephesians 3:16-21 (NIV)

Camp on these verses and pray them as a personal prayer of praise.

HE SUSTAINS ME

"And God is able to make all grace abound toward you, that you, always having all sufficiency in all things, will abound in every good work." 2 Corinthians 9:8 (NIV)

THE HOLY TRINITY

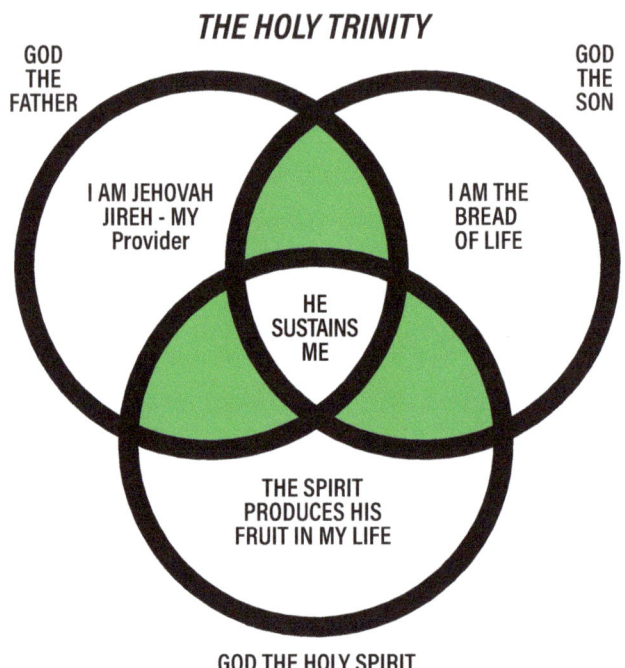

"The fruit of the Spirit is love, joy, peace, patience, kindness, goodness, faithfulness, gentleness, self-control."
Galatians 5:22,23 (NIV)

CHAPTER EIGHT

HE HEALS ME

GOD'S NAMES. GOD'S NATURE. GOD'S PROMISES.

CHAPTER EIGHT

Section One

God the Father - Jehovah Rapha
The LORD my healer

God the Father is declared Jehovah Rapha, the LORD who heals, in Exodus 15. The story is astounding in that the Israelites had just experienced a huge miracle. They were finally escaping the cruel rule of the Egyptians. Running for their lives, with the Egyptian army at their heels, they came to the uncrossable Red Sea. Surely, they would be taken captive again and receive even harsher treatment at the hands of their captors. The amazing story is recorded in Exodus 14. God miraculously came to their rescue by parting the Red Sea, so they actually crossed on dry land! As the enemy pursued them onto the dry seabed the waters crashed back down, saving the Israelites in a mighty fashion!

We pick up the story a mere three days later as they wander away from the Red Sea. They are in desperate need of a drink. Finally, they come upon some water, only to find it is bitter and undrinkable. The Israelites quickly forget how God rescued them with the Red Sea miracle and, not seeking God's help, they murmur and complain to and about Moses. Moses cried out to God for help and God instructed him to throw a particular piece of wood into the water and the water was restored. God again did a miracle for them, and the bitter water became sweet.

The LORD God spoke and instructed the people to listen carefully to Him, to follow Him carefully and none of the diseases bestowed on the Egyptians would befall them. The LORD declared, **"I am the LORD who heals you".** Exodus 15:26 (NIV). God, in His kindness was saying that if they followed Him carefully, He would be their God and the One who would be there to heal them. He would be their rescue.

God's proclamation of His name, Healer, also points to God the Son, the coming Jesus who would offer us healing from all the things that threaten to drag us down.

In Isaiah 61 we read of the **Healer** whose coming was foretold. His very coming would offer healing to the brokenhearted. He would come and proclaim freedom for those who were held captive, and He would bring release from darkness for those imprisoned. He would bring beauty out of ashes and the oil of joy for those who were mourning. What a picture of healing this is!

This scripture in Isaiah 61 details with great accuracy, the things that drag us down. All of us are familiar with them to one degree or another throughout life. The words paint a picture of hearts that can be broken by situations and people, habits we just cannot shake that hold us captive. There may even be shadows or secrets that keep one hiding from freedom and joy. It says that this One, who's coming was foretold here, will come to bring beauty out of ashes. We get ashes when something is burned up, destroyed, unable to be rebuilt. Sometimes we may even strike the match ourselves. Yet there is hope that beauty can arise from the ashes. God is promising the healing oil of joy poured over all the wounds that life can bring. This is a foreshadowing of Jesus Christ.

In Luke 4:17-21 we find the account of Jesus in the temple, reading this very scripture in Isaiah 61 from the temple scrolls. After reading it Jesus announced that this day this very scripture was fulfilled in their hearing. Jesus was declaring that He would be the One who would bring spiritual healing.

Physical healing in our bodies is often God's gift. Yet healing the broken hearted, bringing freedom from the things that hold us captive, bringing light and release from darkness is the promise of our Healer.

This points to Jesus who declared,
"I AM the Light of the world".

Section Two

GOD THE SON

The Light of the World

*"I am the light of the world.
Whoever follows me will never walk in darkness,
but will have the light of life." John 8:12 (NIV)*

God the Son, Jesus, declared Himself as the Light of the world. John 1:5 (NIV) tells us, **"The light shines in the darkness, and the darkness has not overcome it."**

Though we live in a beautiful world, we are also aware that it is a broken world. The daily world news, or a look into hidden abuses of all kinds quickly confirms the brokenness around us. We are also aware of the darkness within that can surface and threaten to overcome us. Discouragement is a wedge in the door of our hearts that can keep the light out. Jesus makes a promise that whoever follows Him will never walk in darkness. He calls us forward, out of the things that hold us and drag us down. He calls us to His presence. He calls us to His word and to prayer, and to the healing of our hearts. He calls us to the Light as He calls us to Himself. He shines in us and through us.

**"Your word is a lamp for my feet, and a light on my path."
Psalm 119:105 (NIV)
"In your light we see light". Psalm 36:9 (NIV)**

A snapshot from our photo album

We spent a Christmas in the high Arctic when John was flying there. It was a surreal experience. The twenty-four-hour darkness was amazing. I admire the people who resiliently live all winter in the dark. At the edge of the village, I was intrigued by a huge shadow cast across the houses in the moonlight. A very large iceberg had been shoved ashore and it loomed in the darkness.

Turning to the other direction in the little village I was drawn to the tiny church in the center of the community. It was outlined in Christmas lights and was a welcome and delightful sight in the darkness.

When we feel the shadows of darkness fall across our paths, we are not helpless nor alone. Jesus came to push back the darkness and to bring us into His light of freedom. Colossians 1 records a powerful prayer which highlights God's plan of rescue and the redemption that Jesus brings as we are transferred from darkness into His Light.

We make the choice to invite Jesus to bring His Light into our lives. The LORD does the work in us. The Father planned for our rescue. Jesus offers His love and grace to us even as we struggle in the dark. The Spirit of God provides His power so that we can live and move in freedom.

God's word reminds us that how we live is determined by our heart and what we think. Proverbs 23:7 (NASB) says, **_"For as he thinks within himself, so he is."_**

It is important to pay attention to what goes on in our hearts and minds. God sheds light on the thoughts that drag us down as we ask Him to help us and as we ponder His word. One of the things I was taught as a young adult has served me well through life. It is about the agreements we make.

It is important to take note of the things we are agreeing with in our hearts and minds. When we agree with negativity, impossibility and a host of discouragements that are unique to our own individual lives, we make agreements with darkness. Examples of these shadowy thoughts would be negative things about ourselves or about the hopelessness around us, the things that make us feel disheartened and worried.

When we camp on those thoughts, we are making agreements that can pull the blinds down on the light of Jesus and on the power and strength He brings to our lives. We begin to feel that God is far away, and a dullness can settle into our hearts as our minds camp on the negative.

When we find ourselves walking in the shadows of darkness with discouragements and disappointments as our common companions, we can turn to Jesus and invite His light to penetrate. Darkness cannot extinguish the light of one small candle or one small flame of hope. Jesus is our healer. He meets us where we are and pulls up the blinds in our hearts and minds so that we can see the light of His strength and power.

He helps us to see the agreements that we have been making. Intentionally turning to Jesus helps us recover the agreements with Him and the promises of Light that He alone can bring into our hearts and minds. Sometimes it is praise music, or a quiet time in His presence letting thankfulness surface. Sometimes it is praying with someone. It takes intentionality.

Sometimes it is finding a trusted person to confide in and seek Godly counsel from. As we review the promises of who God is and how His character changes our character, we focus on all His power and might available to us. God's word, scripture, is powerful as we agree with His promises from the Bible.

*"**Above all else, guard your heart, for everything you do flows from it**."*

Proverbs 4:23 (NIV)

We live in a beautiful world, but it takes intentionality to look for and find the beauty because there is also disease and death, discouragement and disappointment. Even evil is not hard to identify. These will not be fully overcome until eternity, yet when we take responsibility for our own inner lives and invite Jesus into the dark places and the shadows that drag us down, He brings His light. He heals the deep places within. He brings beauty out of ashes. As we guard our hearts, knowing that is the spring from which all of life flows, Jesus works in us bringing greater health and wholeness.

> ## PAUSE & PONDER
>
> *Are there any negative, destructive or hopeless agreements that you have been making in your heart and mind? As individuals we are always growing or regressing. Rarely do we stay in the same place. As we choose our thoughts and what we give permission to settle into our hearts, we find ourselves moving in that direction.*
>
> *Choose life and talk with Jesus about how you want to move forward in your inner life, allowing His healing and Light to bring you to new and fresh places.*
>
> *Be aware of the agreements you make this week. Invite Jesus into your thoughts and the emotions of your heart. This is what it means to "take very thought captive unto the obedience of Christ." (2 Corinthians 10:5) The result can be remarkable and transforming.*

Section Three

GOD THE HOLY SPIRIT

The Spirit of Freedom

God the Holy Spirit gives us the Spirit of wisdom and revelation so that we may know Him better. Ephesians1:17-23 details the light on our journey as we enter into the healing place of God's love. There we find His love to rescue us, Jesus' presence to redeem us, and the Spirit's revelation to walk in the light of His healing and victory.

"I keep asking that the God of our Lord Jesus Christ, the glorious Father, may give you the Spirit of wisdom and revelation, so that you may know him better.

I pray that the eyes of your heart may be enlightened in order that you may know:

- *the hope to which he has called you,*
- *the riches of his glorious inheritance in his holy people,*
- *and his incomparably great power for us who believe.*

That power is the same as the mighty strength God exerted when he raised Christ from the dead and seated him at his right hand in the heavenly realms, far above all rule and authority, power and dominion, and every name that is invoked, not only in the present age but also in the one to come.

And God placed all things under his feet and appointed him to be head over everything for the church, which is his body, the fullness of him who fills everything in every way."
Ephesians 1:17-23 (NIV)

As we intentionally seek to know Him better, the Holy Spirit gives us wisdom and revelation. Our eyes are opened to see the hope that the light of Jesus offers to us.

We begin to see the riches that God offers us as His love **rescues** us, bringing us into union with Him. Our eyes are opened to see the **restoration** that Jesus brings to our hearts as He dispels the darkness and transfers us into His light, healing our brokenness.

We see the beauty in being a part of God's family, sharing with others who are exploring this transformation of the healing of our hearts and minds. We begin to experience the incomparable power of living in the Kingdom of God's Son as His Spirit **reveals** God's wisdom to us.

"He has rescued us from the domain of darkness, and transferred us to the kingdom of His beloved Son, in whom we have redemption, the forgiveness of sins." Colossians 1:13,14 (NASB)

A snapshot from my life

It happened during a season when I served as Women's Pastor in a mid-sized church in our denomination. We had a small team of dedicated, praying women who took seriously the privilege of praying for one another and for individual women who came forward to seek God's healing.

Whenever someone asked for some inner healing prayer, the ladies team came "prayed up", depending on Jehovah Rapha to guide the time of prayer. It was always a special time together. Often there was a beautiful release as forgiveness was offered and the burdens of the past were released to God, to let Him carry what was cast off that day. The penetrating darkness lifted, and newfound joy was often the result.

Sometimes though, we found that the newfound joy one experienced diminished as time went on, and some of the struggles resurfaced. Our small team began to pray and asked the Lord for wisdom and guidance, for His light on this pathway when darkness seemed to creep back in.

"For with you is the fountain of life; in your light we see light". Psalm 36:9

I was reminded of a time when John was working on the ceiling of an airport hangar. A tiny fragment of metal flew into his eye. He finally got in to see the doctor. His eye was frozen, and the piece of metal was removed. As the eye healed it was clear that something was still not right. His vision was blurred. The doctor checked again and told us that while the metal was in the eye, there had been enough time for a small rust ring to develop. This was causing the blurred vision and now that rust ring needed to be removed. Once that was done, the eye healed back to normal.

I felt this story was brought back to my mind right then for a reason. It seemed clear to us that the release of the past to God and the sincere forgiveness offered was complete in the times we prayed with those seeking healing prayer.

That had been like the metal being removed from the eye. It was gone, but did a "rust ring" remain?

The rust ring was like the things we can begin to believe about ourselves as a result of actions against us, even long ago. Even with forgiveness settled, the lies of shame and blame that we have owned can remain. When we acknowledge the negative agreements that we have made about ourselves, the rust ring of shame can be removed. We can then see ourselves clearly, as God sees us, fully loved and fully accepted.

Once we learned this, we could pray through the agreements, and we found another whole layer of healing

emerged for the one seeking healing. With the agreements broken, light dispelled the darkness! God is so good.
Freedom was found.

If the old patterns of thinking came back, now there was a tool
in the toolbox to recognize the agreements and choose healing.

**We serve an amazing God who rescues, redeems
and reveals!**

Section Four

Take Heart

When difficult things happen in life, it is easy to wonder where God is and to ask how God, if He truly loved us, could allow this.

Scripture tells us that in this world we will have trouble. (John 16:33) Even Jesus felt forsaken by God the Father when the cross was in front of Him. Yet victory was also just beyond the cross at the empty grave. Jesus told His followers, ***Take heart! For I have overcome the world". John 16:33 (NIV)***

We see brokenness around us. Hurting people hurt people. Self-seekers ignore others and put themselves first, often even at the peril of others. Evil tries to trample fairness and goodness. Injustice often overshadows justice. Illness and death are often unwelcome and untimely intruders. It is tempting to blame God and run from Him in our pain.

Yet in the midst of it all, God is present to heal our hearts. He loves us. In the midst of it all Jesus cares and gives us His light in our hearts to help us "take heart" and overcome what seeks to drag us down. His Spirit fills us with wisdom and with revelation that comes from above.

As we pause and acknowledge His presence with us, as we trust His love even in the dark, He gives us a firm place on which to stand. He gives a peace that passes all understanding. The Bible explains it. I call it the circle effect.

There is a cycle that happens in our lives as we choose to bring God into focus throughout our day.

Here is one of my favorite examples of this beautiful cyclical effect.

As we already know, God's word tells us,

> ***"Above all else, guard your heart,***

For everything you do flows from it." Proverbs 4:23 (NIV)

Being the gatekeeper of our own heart means being careful about which attitudes we nurse, what thoughts we allow to make paths in our minds, and what images and words we allow to be deposited there. The essence of our lives springs from our hearts and what we focus on. When a heart is at peace, peace springs from within. When we allow anxiety, anger, edginess, unresolved hurts and negative thoughts to live there, that is what springs forth. Our entire lives are affected by the wellspring of our hearts. It is our individual responsibility to tend our own heart carefully and wisely.

God doesn't leave us alone in this task of guarding our hearts. He offers us His help in this. He tells us that He, Himself will guard our hearts and minds with His peace. He tells us what to do. He gives us a key.

"Rejoice in the Lord always. I will say it again: Rejoice!

"Let your gentleness be evident to all. The Lord is near.

"Do not be anxious about anything, but in every situation, by prayer and petition, with thanksgiving, present your requests to God.

"And the peace of God, which transcends all understanding, will guard your hearts and your minds in Christ Jesus."

Philippians 4:4-7 (NIV)

Thanksgiving is the key.

It is not simply "having an attitude of gratitude" and looking for the good in things. No, it is much deeper than that. **It flows from a rejoicing in who the LORD is,** rejoicing that He is near, rejoicing that He is with us in every situation. It is giving thanks for who He is with us, and in us, right where we are walking.

Even in the midst of all the things we feel anxious about, God instructs us not to focus there. He calls us to focus first on Him, to rejoice in Him! Then He instructs us to bring our requests to Him, in everything, with this thanksgiving for Him flowing from our hearts.

It sounds impossible to be thankful in everything. Yet as we turn our eyes from the circumstances and challenges swirling around us, and lift our eyes to Him, our focus becomes the LORD rather than the struggles.

We need not be thankful FOR everything, but scripture tells us we can be thankful IN everything. Our requests change as we move from desperate "please, please" prayers for the outcomes we want, to "thank you, thank you" prayers for who He is, with us, through the struggles.

God the Father is our Healer. He heals our hearts in the midst of broken places. God the Son is our Light. He brings His peace and His presence to walk with us through any struggle. He is closer than our own breath. God the Spirit brings His wisdom and revelation as we move through sometimes confusing and chaotic times.

As we bring our thanksgiving to God for who He is, and as we present our requests to Him, trusting Him, relying on Him, on His love and the strength of His character, *He promises to guard our hearts AND our anxious minds with His peace, which is beyond our understanding. It is supernatural!*

What a beautiful circle of faith this is!

We guard our hearts, being thankful for who He is in us as we pray, being careful what we let take up residence within us and leaving our anxious concerns and outcomes in God's hands. And God guards our hearts and our minds with His supernatural peace.

Trust and peace go hand in hand. We bring one, and God provides the other.

No God...No Peace
Know God...Know Peace

Peace that surpasses all understanding!

"May the God of hope fill you with all joy and peace
as you trust in him,
so that you may overflow with hope by the power of the
Holy Spirit."

Romans 15:13 (NIV)

Our part is to trust Him. His part is all the rest, to fill us with hope, overflowing by the power of His Spirit. That is true healing.

The matter of "making agreements" is important in our day-to-day life. We are often unaware that it is even happening. We can feel inadequate, overwhelmed and helpless, or just anxious in areas or circumstances and situations in which we find ourselves as we let shadows darken our thoughts. We know from Scripture that there really is an enemy of God, an enemy of our souls as we seek out God's presence in our lives. This enemy seeks to devour. (1 Peter 5:8 NIV)

The world offers remedies for such times of depletion, and they may work for awhile. Yet the well of self is a shallow well and there often comes a point when we simply feel consumed, devoured, empty, with nothing left to draw on from our own resources.

As Christians, we turn to God's word and God's presence. We can draw from His well that has no end. We can draw from the depth of who God is as He offers His presence and power to us and in us. (2 Peter 1:3 & 4)

I keep this tool of "agreements" handy, and if I find reactions of my own, or others, are simply out of scope to the issue at hand, I look to see what agreements are being made. I ask God to help me respond in the opposite spirit with the help of His Holy Spirit and I seek to turn to rejoicing in who He is with me and in me as I walk.

PAUSE & PONDER

Am I making agreements in my heart and mind, believing things about myself that are contrary to God's character and His powerful names over me?

How can I respond in the opposite spirit by the power of the Holy Spirit and make agreements with what God offers me of Himself as I grow to understand who He is?

He is the LORD our Healer.

He is the One who brings light into the darkness.

He is the One who gives us His Spirit of wisdom and revelation.

A prayer to pray as my own

Heavenly Father,

Today I am so grateful that You are my healer. You are the one who puts Your salve of comfort on my heart when I need it. You help me to forgive so that the disease of bitter unforgiveness cannot take over my mind and body.

You can redeem that which has been broken, whether by my own hand or by others. You pardon, purify and cleanse me. Thank you, Lord!

Too often we walk limping, when Your grace can bring healing to our minds and hearts. Inward healing is our first need, Lord. Please reveal, by Your Spirit, any "rust ring" that blurs my vision. Thank you for Your kindness.

Thank you that You also care about my physical state and are able to bring healing to my body. Grant the doctors divine wisdom in providing care. Grant me understanding in seeking to maintain wellness and lead me to wholeness.

You are my God of Hope. By Your Spirit and through Your Word You counsel me. I trust You to be at work in my life, filling me up and bringing Your light and healing into the dark places.

Fill me with Your joy and peace. May I rejoice in all You are for all of me. Today I put my life, my health and all that is "me" into Your loving hands. I give You my faith and trust, believing that You will walk every step with me today.

May Your presence surround me, and Your Spirit comfort me. O Lord, You are my healer in every sense of the word. Thank you that You are my Light in the darkness, and You give me wisdom and revelation. I praise Your name today with thanksgiving. Amen.

Release everyone and everything to Him. Trust Him. You will find all you need in His presence.

> **PAUSE & PONDER**
>
> *Is there someone or something you want to release to God right now, trusting Him to carry the concern and the weight of it as you find all you need in His presence?*

As we daily release everything and everyone in our lives to God, we will begin to be more aware of His presence in us, and in our relationships and situations. We will begin to be more aware of the agreements we are making as we navigate our days.

A good key to awareness is to notice when we are feeling and sensing a leaning toward hopelessness. It is then we can trust the God of Hope to fill us with joy and peace. Though nothing may change around us, His Spirit at work in us changes us on the inside, bringing hope and comfort as we face any challenges that may come. He is the healer of our hearts and minds and of the wounds, both internal and external.

A Christian friend or counsellor can be a help and a blessing if we need someone to pray with. Going into His presence together in prayer is what believers do with and for one another.

He brings Light into the darkness.
He brings hope and He brings healing.
We can trust Him completely.

I am encased in His presence and in His freedom!

Jehovah Rapha - My Healer

"So if the Son sets you free, you will be free indeed." John 8:36 (NIV)

"Now the Lord is the Spirit, and where the Spirit of the Lord is,
there is freedom." 2 Corinthians 3:17 (NIV)

THE HOLY TRINITY

GOD THE FATHER

GOD THE SON

I AM JEHOVAH RAPHA - The LORD my Healer

I AM THE LIGHT OF THE WORLD

HE GIVES ME FREEDOM

THE SPIRIT OF WISDOM AND REVELATION

GOD THE HOLY SPIRIT

He gives me freedom.
"May the God of hope fill you with all joy and peace as You trust in him, so that you may overflow with hope by the power of the Holy Spirit." Romans 15:13 (NIV)

CHAPTER NINE

HE GIVES ME HIS PEACE

GOD'S NAMES. GOD'S NATURE. GOD'S PROMISES.

CHAPTER NINE

The LORD my peace

SECTION ONE
God the Father - Jehovah Shalom
The LORD my peace

We all define peace differently. For some it might mean a quiet place, an absence of something annoying, a type of beautiful music, a special spot or even the absence of conflict.

When God is referred to as **"The LORD is peace"** it carries a much deeper meaning than an outward condition.

God the Father - Jehovah Shalom

Judges 6 tells us the fascinating story of Gideon. It happened in a time when Israel was once again under siege. A once-defeated enemy, the Midianites, were fiercely attacking the Israelite people who were terrified. They had once again chosen other gods to worship, forgetting the miracles and rescue of Jehovah God that they had experienced first-hand.

Again, under such dire conditions of war, they were fleeing to the hills and calling out for God to save them once again. Gideon was hiding in the threshing barn, threshing some wheat to keep it from the Midianites. An angel of the Lord sat down under a tree and spoke to Gideon. "The LORD is with you, mighty warrior." Gideon replied, "Pardon me?"

Gideon asked why, if the LORD was with them, had all this hardship happened to them. It felt as if God had abandoned them. The angel told Gideon to go in the strength he had and save the Israelites out of the hand of the enemy. Gideon argued with the angel that his clan was the weakest and that he was the least in his family! The LORD told Gideon that He would be with him, and Gideon would see victory. The story is amazing in its detail. Gideon made a sacrifice to the LORD and then he asked for a sign that he really was hearing correctly.

He asked twice, once that a sheep fleece on the ground would be wet with dew and all the ground around dry. And then again that the opposite would happen. God confirmed the sign. This is where we get the phrase, "Putting out a fleece" when we are seeking clarity from God in hesitant faith.

The LORD said to Gideon, "Peace! You are not going to die". So, Gideon built an altar of worship to the LORD and called it, **"The LORD is peace."**

I especially like God's gentle dealing with Gideon. He doesn't reprimand him for asking for the sign of the fleece. He instructs Gideon to reduce his army drastically and God knows this will frighten Gideon as the enemy army is huge. So God also instructs him to sneak down and listen in at the enemy camp where he hears an account of a dream detailing the Israelites victory. With courage he goes forth with his small army and has a miraculous victory!

The LORD is peace! The LORD brought peace to the Israelites. This story is an arrow that points to Jesus in John 14 when He says, "My peace I give you, do not be troubled or afraid."

Walking in the LORD's peace is a mixture of both courage and humility, seeking understanding beyond our own limited grasp. Gideon's courage would have seemed fool-hardy and reckless had he not had the humility to approach God in trust and confidence. Apart from God, Gideon could do nothing. Without God's peace, he was troubled and afraid.

The elements of Gideon's story contain fear, doubt, lack of confidence, hesitant believing, miraculous signs, growing courage, worship, obedience and victory. I love the flow of God's love, Gideon's growing courage and trust and God's miraculous victory.

Though God's people often suffered the consequences of turning away from Him, His love rescued them over and over, flowing redeeming peace to His children.

PAUSE & PONDER

Following God's ways and His instructions can seem to make no sense at times. Can you recall a time when you needed God's courage and confirmation to follow Him in faith?

**"You will keep in perfect peace
those whose minds are steadfast,
because they trust in you." Isaiah 26:3 (NIV)**

<u>Section Two</u>

<u>GOD THE SON</u>

I AM The True Vine

In John 15 where Jesus says, "Without Me you can do nothing", He is explaining how we are likened to the branch on a grape vine. Without the flow of life-giving nourishment from the vine to the branch, there would be no fruit. Jesus calls it "abiding".

In the same way, without our connection to Jesus, the True vine, our lives would be fruitless. Years ago, when I first read the phrase, "without me you can do nothing", I argued with it in my mind. There was lots I could do. Opportunities avail all around. Yet as I sat with it, I realized Jesus was referring to spiritual fruit. Without Him my life would bear no fruit of eternal value. Oh, I could be busy and productive, but the sweet fruit of things of eternal value would be missing. And those things, I find, are the things that bring the greatest satisfaction.

To keep that life-flow going, I need to be vulnerable as Gideon was,

telling God my fears and insecurities, my doubts and at times, my hesitant believing. I need to come to Him in worship and with courage to follow Him. Faith can be complex. Relationships with other believers and even within the church can be messy. As we work through the complexities, the hurts and the heartaches, the joys and the blessings, we fight for our faith. Many choose to discard their faith when complexity arises rather than fight for it. Yet the fight is so worth it! A simplicity arises above the confusion that lets us sit with the mystery, being blessed with His presence, experiencing His peace, as we offer our questions to Him as our offering of trust. It even lets us leave those who have hurt us, off the hook and in God's hand, knowing that He works out all things for our good and His glory. (Romans 8:28)

Staying connected to the True Vine is where life-giving hope and peace flow. It is remarkable. It is truly life-giving and the source of true peace.

If I let His words of truth from the Bible "continue to be present" in my life, applying them to my heart and my actions, then His words abide in me, and His truth transforms my life.

When God's Word is a continuing presence in my life, guiding my thoughts, actions and attitudes, then my prayers will be different from the self-centered requests for which I often beg God. The results will be for eternity.

These verses also say that God prunes the vine. I once read an insight from Andrew Murray, one of the great Jesus followers from the past. He said that God's pruning knife is His word and as we let His word shape us it will result in greater fruitfulness.

Our fulfillment in this life comes as we bear fruit for God's kingdom. Keeping God's Word central in our hearts and lives allows His words to "continue to be present". It allows the Spirit of Counsel to speak to us as we walk out our faith in "who my God is"!

Many things distract us from God's word in our lives. It is easy to let its importance diminish. As it fades from our focus and other things take greater precedence, I find that deep inner peace erodes as well. A casual read, a short devotional or a quick verse here and there is helpful and God, in His kindness, will speak through those. But as any relationship slowly erodes when we let its importance to us slip away amidst the clamor of life, so will our walk with God slowly erode as we skip time to connect with Him, read His word and talk with Him. We will find our peace and content-ment eroding as well.

I have found that the hope, when we find ourselves in that place of quiet discontent, is to know God is only one good prayer time away. Just as a long overdue visit with a good friend can re-establish our connection, so taking the time to be still before God and focusing on Him can draw us from the distractions. As we invite Him into our situations and complexities, letting His love wash over us, He changes our perspective, settles our hearts and draws us back to the peace that trusting Him brings as we release everything and everyone to Him.

> We sat around our backyard fire pit. As we watched the stars come out, we talked about how to walk out our faith on a day-to-day basis. We talked about what the Bible had to say about business ethics, raising a family, dealing with church politics or prickly people. At the end of many of our discussions our friend, Jerry, would say, "It really all comes down to abiding". Having good friends who pursue the journey of following Jesus with us is truly a gift. At the end of an evening of discussion whether around the fire pit or around our living room fireplace, we often voiced our collective concerns in prayer. Jerry would refrain from offering God solutions to the things we were challenged with. Instead, he would pray, "LORD, establish Your kingdom in our families, our work ..." or in whatever else we had talked about that evening. We often ended on that word "abiding".

I still keep coming back to that, abiding. It truly is the answer to walking out our Christian faith where the rubber meets the road on a Monday morning. His flow of life and peace to us as we stay connected to Him.

John 15 describes the picture clearly of the branch attached to the vine and producing much sweet fruit.

Jesus reminds us that He is the vine, and we are the branches. It is only when the power of the Holy Spirit flows through us that we are able to experience His peace and touch lives with His love. A life changed by Jesus' love is the fruit produced. Apart from Him we can do nothing of any eternal value.

Then Jesus goes on to say something truly amazing:

"If you abide in me, and my words abide in you, you shall ask what you will, and it shall be done unto you. Herein is my Father glorified, that you bear much fruit; so shall you be my disciples." John 15:7 & 8 (KJV)

The result is clear. My abiding in Christ will even affect my prayers. In the original Greek this word "abide" means to remain or "continue to be present".

If I "continue to be present" with Christ and make time in His presence a priority, I abide in Him. As I seek Him and His Word daily, in each decision I encounter, I abide in Him and His wisdom and discernment guide me and abide in me.

"Continue to be present".
It does take effort, attention and intentionality,
just as any valued relationship takes conscious tending.
It is our daily choice.
Being present with God, dialoguing with Him in prayer, is
the oxygen of our soul and our very place of true peace.

PAUSE & PONDER

When you feel a little breathless it is good to remember that prayer is the oxygen of the believer's life. Breathe in His presence. Breathe out your cares and concerns and confessions. He is only one good prayer time away.

Section Three

GOD THE HOLY SPIRIT

The Spirit of Counsel

The Spirt of Counsel is God's Holy Spirit giving us His wisdom as He nudges our hearts and minds through the pruning of God's word. As we commit our way to Him and trust Him to guide us, He gives divine insight.

Psalm 32:8 (NKJV) tells us, **"I will instruct you and teach you in the way you should go; I will guide you with My eye."** Most of us can recall "the look" our parents could give us across a room. It might be an encouraging, "Go for it! You've got this." It might be a look of caution, or a "Don't you dare" look. Their counsel could silently reach across a room. It was our choice as to how we received it.

God's Spirit can counsel us through His word as we pause in His presence to receive His counsel. It is our choice as to how we receive it.

There are times when we don't want God's counsel. We want His hand to dispense exactly what we are praying for, according to our own immediate best solutions. God's peace is a marker in our lives. When His peace is lacking, we know we can go back to His presence and seek His counsel. His counsel will never disagree with His word. They go hand-in-hand. His counsel will bring peace when we make the choice to follow His direction.

Gideon experienced the counsel of God in the Old Testament. Jesus calls us to be connected to Him in a way that brings life-giving hope and counsel into our lives. And the Spirit gives counsel as we keep our hearts soft and our posture leaning in to listen to His still, small voice.

Trusting God to speak, to lead, to continually supply the life-giving hope and direction from the Spirit of Counsel comes as we abide, staying connected to the True Vine daily. It's the place of real peace.

"But we have this treasure in jars of clay to show that this all- surpassing power is from God and not from us." 2 Corinthians 4:7 (NIV)

"The LORD delights in those who fear him, who put their hope in his unfailing love." Psalm 147:11 (NIV)

He is always only a prayer away.

Truly, the LORD delights in those who fear Him, who stand in reverent awe of His immense power and might and who put their trust in His unfailing, reliable love. To them He gives His peace.

"But blessed is the one who trusts in the LORD, whose confidence is in him. They will be like a tree planted by the water that sends out its roots by the stream. It does not fear when heat comes; its leaves are always green. It has no worries in a year of drought and never fails to bear fruit." Jeremiah 17:7 & 8 (NIV)

Confidence in the LORD = PEACE

Peace can vanish from our souls like an ice cube on a hot day. A conversation, a news story, a bank balance, an email or letter in the mail, a meeting with the boss, any number of things can quickly steal our peace.

We have more control in what we let into our hearts than we often realize.

God gives us instructions that show the way.

"Peace I leave with you; my peace I give you. I do not give to you as the world gives. Do not let your hearts be troubled and do not be afraid." John 14:27 (NIV)

The "Let not" is so much easier said than done.
But God tells us how to do it.

"Let the peace of Christ rule in your hearts, since as members of one body you were called to peace. And be thankful." Colossians 3:15 (NIV)

PAUSE AND PONDER

Today, when someone or something brings angst to your heart and your peace vanishes in the wind, pause and be thankful. Be thankful, not necessarily for the thing that is distressing, but be thankful IN it. Thank God for His amazing presence, power and peace to walk you through. Thank Him that He is the God of Peace and the true source of Peace for your soul.

When our hearts are troubled, we can remember His "let not" and turn to who He is with thanksgiving, to "let" His peace wash over us as we give thanks for who He is in us, in our situation.

Our confidence is in Him!

A prayer to pray as my Own

Father God,

Thank you for Your peace that passes all understanding. Thank you for the waterfall of Your grace and for Your presence in and with me.

Fan the desire in my heart to read Your Word. Make it clear to me so that it will guide my thoughts and my actions. Reveal to me the treasures in Your Word. Cause me to pursue it more than silver or gold or any other thing, for Your words are life to my soul. They bring Your peace to my heart as Your Spirit counsels me and as I thank You for who You are in the middle of my circumstances. Help me keep my eyes on You, LORD, and off the swirling question marks of the day.

Direct my steps, my plans, my thoughts and my actions as I navigate the maze of life. Thank you that You know the way through, and in that I find my peace.

I love You, LORD, and I'm so thankful for who You are in my life today! In the strong name of Jesus I pray, amen.

PAUSE & PONDER

As you ask God to remind you to take note of what you "let" and "let not" into your heart today, always return to thanksgiving for who our great God is! It changes our perspective and helps make the way for God's goodness to be evident.

He gives me His peace

"But blessed is the one who trusts in the Lord,

Whose confidence is in him.

They will be like a tree planted by the water

that sends its roots by the stream.

It does not fear when heat comes; its leaves are always green.

It has no worries in a year of drought and never fails to bear fruit."

Jeremiah 17:7 & 8

THE HOLY TRINITY

HIS PEACE – MY FIRM PLACE TO STAND

The 23rd Psalm contains all seven of the Redemptive Names of God

The Lord is my shepherd; **Jehovah Raah –
Good Shepherd**
I shall not want. **Jehovah Jireh – My Provider**

He makes me to lie down in green pastures;
He leads me beside the still waters.

He restores my soul; **Jehovah Rapha – My Healer**

He leads me in the paths of righteousness for His
name's sake.
Jehovah Tsidkinu- My Righteousness.

Yea, though I walk through the valley of the shadow
of death,
I will fear no evil;
For You are with me; **Jehovah Shammah – God with us**
Your rod and Your staff, they comfort me.

You prepare a table before me in the presence of my
enemies; **Jehovah Nissi – My Banner**
You anoint my head with oil;

My cup runs over. **Jehovah Shalom – My Peace**
Surely goodness and mercy shall follow me all the days of
my life; and I will dwell in the house of the Lord forever.

ENCASED IN HIS PRESENCE AND HIS HOLINESS

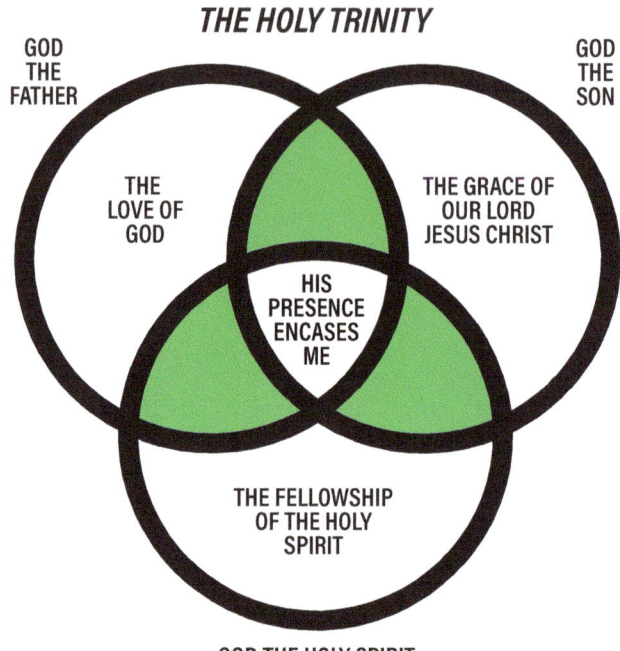

THE HOLY TRINITY

GOD THE FATHER

GOD THE SON

THE LOVE OF GOD

THE GRACE OF OUR LORD JESUS CHRIST

HIS PRESENCE ENCASES ME

THE FELLOWSHIP OF THE HOLY SPIRIT

GOD THE HOLY SPIRIT

**"The grace of the Lord Jesus Christ,
and the love of God,
and the fellowship of the Holy Spirit
be with you all."**

2 Corinthians 13:14

A prayer for all of us from Colossians 1:9b-12 (NIV)

"We continually ask God to fill you with the knowledge of his will through all the wisdom and understanding that the Spirit gives, so that you may live a life worthy of the Lord and please him in every way:

Bearing fruit in every good work, growing in the knowledge of God, being strengthened with all power according to His glorious might so that you may have great endurance and patience, and giving joyful thanks to the Father, who has qualified you to share in the inheritance of his holy people in the kingdom of light." Amen.

Author's note

All references to the Trinity are capitalized.

The thoughts expressed here are based on the author's personal understanding of Scripture and personal life experience. Readers are always encouraged to do their own study of the Bible to confirm their own understanding. As we share with each other, we grow from one another's insights, stories and glimpses of our great God.

**May you be blessed in the name of the Father,
and of the Son,
and of the Holy Spirit
as you walk in all the fullness of The Trinity!**

*"May the grace of the Lord Jesus Christ,
and the love of God,
and the fellowship of the Holy Spirit be with you all."
2 Corinthians 13:14 (NIV)*

"God's Names. God's Nature. God's Promises."

How can this mystery of The Father, Son and Holy Spirit actually make a difference in our lives on an ordinary Monday morning?

Studying the mystery of The Holy Trinity has changed my praying in such an amazing way. My prayers have changed from pleading "Please! Please!" prayers to "Thank you! Thank you!" prayers, creating a depth of awe that grows my confidence in my faith in God!

As I have studied some of the Names of God, the "I AM" statements of Jesus, and the characteristics of the Holy Spirit I have been amazed at how they intersect, merging as One in the Holy Trinity, creating an inexplicable place of peace and security. Here is a very firm place we are invited to by God Himself. Here is a secure resting place, even in the midst of all the uncertainty of life and the question marks that swirl around us.

This is my account of my glimpses of this amazing Three-in-One God. Through the lens of my own experiences, I share this firm place we can all find in The LORD as we navigate trusting Him through changing times.

ABOUT THE AUTHOR

Gail Rodgers is a freelance writer who has a passion for discovering how the Scriptures apply to everyday life. She draws from her experience in the aviation industry where she worked alongside her husband in commercial and private aviation in the Canadian North. Among her many roles she worked as Operations Manager, Controller and Safety Officer.

Gail has also served as a pastor and is an online published devotional writer who enjoys writing and speaking. Gail lives in Alberta, Canada with her husband, John and especially enjoys spending time with her family.

Some of her writings can be found at Thoughts About God. https://thoughtsaboutgod.com/category/gail-rodgers

www.ingramcontent.com/pod-product-compliance
Lightning Source LLC
Jackson TN
JSHW071024270325
81505JS00002B/2